Leadership From the Midd

In the face of a global pandemic, catastrophic weather events, war, racism, and attacks on democracy, how should educational leaders respond? How can leaders enable their schools and districts to be agile, safe, and effective places of learning that help young people develop the knowledge and character that will empower them to shape their futures? While some schools and districts have taken top-down or bottom-up approaches, renowned education scholar Andy Hargreaves explores a new type of leadership – "leadership from the middle" – which becomes a driver of transformational change. Drawing from research with educational leaders across the United States, United Kingdom, and Canada, Hargreaves discusses a type of leadership that regards obstacles as opportunities, embraces leadership paradox, and is collaborative, inspiring, and inclusive. This ground-breaking book unpacks not only what this type of leadership looks like, but also how it is most effective in addressing complex problems and in educating young people to develop diverse global competencies to prepare them for their futures.

Andy Hargreaves is Research Professor at Boston College, USA and Visiting Professor at the University of Ottawa, Canada. He is an elected member of the National Academy of Education. Andy's books have attracted eight Outstanding Writing Awards, he holds three honorary doctorates, and he has been honoured in the United States, United Kingdom, and Canada for services to public education and educational research.

Routledge Leading Change Series

Series Editors: Andy Hargreaves & Pak Tee Ng

The world is crying out loud for quality education, and for the type of leadership and change to make quality education a reality. Never has there been a greater need for grasping the big pictures of leadership and change in education, which creates the world of tomorrow by developing future generations today. This is especially pertinent as we contemplate the disruptions caused by COVID-19 and the education landscape in a post-pandemic world.

In this series, you will find some of the world's leading intellectual authorities on educational leadership and change. From the pens of writers such as Dennis Shirley, Pak Tee Ng, Andy Hargreaves, Michael Fullan, Amanda Datnow, Vicky Park, Santiago Rincón-Gallardo, Armand Doucet, Yong Zhao, and Bill McDiarmid, come wise insights and breakthrough ideas on this subject. They ask what the new imperatives of educational change are. They explore the paradoxical nature of educational change in celebrated Asian cultures and systems like those of Singapore. They point to the power of professional collaboration and leading from the middle in schools, and networks of schools and across the world, rather than just driving change from the top. They invite us to think about and pursue educational change as social movements aimed at liberating learning. They highlight the surreal nature of leadership and change at this critical moment in world history.

This series of books is for the stout-hearted and open-minded reader who is keenly looking for inspiration to unlock the potential of educational leadership and change in this turbulent world.

Published books in the series include:

Learning from Singapore: The Power of Paradoxes
By Pak Tee Ng

Surreal Change: The Real Life of Transforming Public Education
By Michael Fullan

Professional Collaboration with Purpose: Teacher Learning Towards Equitable and Excellent Schools
By Amanda Datnow and Vicki Park

Liberating Learning: Educational Change as Social Movement
By Santiago Rincón-Gallardo

Teaching Life: Our Calling, Our Choices, Our Challenges
By Armand Doucet

Learning for Uncertainty: Teaching Students How to Thrive in a Rapidly Evolving World
By Yong Zhao and Bill McDiarmid

Leadership From the Middle: The Beating Heart of Educational Transformation
By Andy Hargreaves

For more information about this series, please visit: https://www.routledge.com/Routledge-Leading-Change-Series/book-series/RLCS

Leadership From the Middle
The Beating Heart of Educational Transformation

Andy Hargreaves

Routledge
Taylor & Francis Group

NEW YORK AND LONDON

Designed cover image: © Getty Images

First published 2024
by Routledge
605 Third Avenue, New York, NY 10158

and by Routledge
4 Park Square, Milton Park, Abingdon, Oxon, OX14 4RN

Routledge is an imprint of the Taylor & Francis Group, an informa business

© 2024 Andy Hargreaves

ISBN: 978-1-138-92686-8 (hbk)
ISBN: 978-1-138-92687-5 (pbk)
ISBN: 978-1-315-68292-1 (ebk)

DOI: 10.4324/9781315682921

Typeset in Adobe Caslon Pro
by Apex CoVantage, LLC

Contents

About the Author

Andy Hargreaves is Research Professor at Boston College and Visiting Professor at the University of Ottawa. He is an elected member of the National Academy of Education, Past President of the International Congress of School Effectiveness and Improvement, President of the ARC Education Collaboratory, and commissioning editor for the *Journal of Professional Capital and Community*. Andy's books have attracted eight Outstanding Writing Awards – including the 2015 Grawemeyer Award in Education for *Professional Capital* (with Michael Fullan). He has been honoured in the United States, United Kingdom, and Canada for services to public education and educational research. Andy is ranked by *Education Week* as the 2023 #16 scholar with most influence on US education policy debate. He holds honorary doctorates from Uppsala University in Sweden, the Education University of Hong Kong and the University of Bolton in the UK. In 2015, Boston College gave him its Excellence in Teaching with Technology Award.

Andy's most recent books, all with Dennis Shirley, are *The Age of Identity: Who Do Our Kids Think They Are? (Corwin, 2024)*, *Well-being in Schools* (ASCD, 2022) and *Five Paths of Student Engagement* (Solution Tree, 2021). His memoir, *Moving*, of growing up in a working-class community, is published by Solution Tree (2020).

Andy has addressed international conferences for organizations such as the OECD, the World Bank, UNESCO, the International Baccalaureate, Education International, the International Confederation of Principals, the World Education Summit, and the World Education Research Association. He has delivered addresses in over 50 countries, 47 US states, and all Australian states and Canadian provinces.

Preface

Whenever we face a change, or need to change, we look for leaders and we look to their leadership for guidance. We need leaders who show up and step forward when a building has collapsed, when a shooting has happened, or when disease is running rife in our communities. We need leaders who have known what it's like to be hungry, stressed, bereaved, or afraid and can empathize with our own struggles because of that. We crave leadership that can protect us and make us feel safe. Good leaders, great leaders even, give us something to believe in, help us glimpse a better future, and show us how to get there. They lift us up, move us forward, make us end our petty squabbles, and inspire us to work together for a better life for everyone.

Some leaders, like Nelson Mandela and Mahatma Gandhi, bring us peace and reconciliation amidst conflict and hate. Others, like Prime Minister Jacinda Ardern in New Zealand, or President Volodymyr Zelenskyy of Ukraine, have shown calmness, courage, and unflappable resolve in the face of deadly pandemics and horrific wars, respectively. Then there are the everyday heroes: the nurse who saved my grandfather's life when no one else would tend to him during the 1918 flu pandemic, the school leaders who worked every day, including vacations, to get their schools through the next pandemic a century later, and the wartime teachers and professors who keep online learning going for their students from their muddy trenches, or who teach classes in bombed-out buildings and subterranean shelters.

We all need leadership like this from time to time – leadership that exhibits courage and persistence in acts of selfless sacrifice that better the lives of others. Whether they are famous politicians, inspiring teachers, or life-changing mentors, we can all recall standout individuals like these. Wherever heroic leadership exists, we must value and not disparage it. But we cannot rely on individual heroism alone. By its very nature, this kind of leadership is morally as well as mathematically exceptional.

If we are surrounded by uncertainty, confronted with seemingly endless crises, and overwhelmed by the sheer scale of what lies before us, we must turn to the power of the many, and not rely on the superhuman qualities of the few. When hostile enemies invade us, when pandemics spread sickness and fever among us, when the effects of climate change can strike at any time with fires, floods, and famine, and when schools find themselves turned upside down and inside out with the consequences of all these forces, we can no longer depend on leadership at the top. We must turn elsewhere instead, to leaders who are greater in number, closer to the action, more in tune with local circumstances, and more able to mobilize people they know and trust in response to the changes that confront them. This is the kind of leadership that this book addresses – what I call *Leadership From the Middle*.

This is not my first book about leadership. In 2006, I published *Sustainable Leadership*, one of my other two books on the subject, with Dean Fink.[1] This book was based on research in eight secondary schools and their experiences of change over 30 years to try and determine what distinguished change that was sustainable from change that was not. In addition to our data, we drew on theory in science, ecology, biodiversity, organizational management, and sociology to understand not just what made changes sustainable or not, but what sustainable leadership meant, and involved. Sustainable leadership, we argued, has seven components. It focuses on things that matter. It persists over time. It requires collective responsibility. It must not have a negative impact on other schools and communities in the surrounding environment. It prospers from diverse environments and leadership teams. It renews rather than depletes people's energy. And it conserves the best of the past in moving forward to a stronger future. Sustainable leadership is more relevant than ever now in an era of climate change, pandemics, inequality, and racial conflicts.[2] The importance of thinking and leading sustainably reappears in this book too, especially in Chapter 5.

Leadership From the Middle – my third book on leadership, and the eighth book in the Routledge *Leading Change* series that I edit with Pak Tee Ng – has been inspired by a long-running collaborative study with ten school district leaders in Ontario, Canada, as well as experiences with supporting and investigating school-to-school collaborations and school networks in Canada, the United States, and the United Kingdom. Its message is simple. Leading everything in detail from the top is undesirable when there is ideological and even tyrannical control. It is also no longer useful in policy environments that have abandoned implementing relatively straightforward and achievable goals to improve test-based performance in literacy and mathematics in favour of developing diverse global competencies in knowledge, skills, and well-being. Bottom-up leadership, meanwhile, may throw up interesting innovations, but it creates inconsistency, disproportionately serves innovators in privileged communities who get more latitude for creativity, and places schools at the mercy of individualized initiatives and market forces.

So, as with many things, when we are faced with extremes, of Left and Right, or top and bottom, the answer is somewhere in the middle. But that's just the start. The next question is what should that middle look like? Several writers who work with whole school systems think of leadership in this respect as leading *in* the middle. The middle, for them, is a tier, layer, or level that connects the top to the bottom. It doesn't change or transform anything. It just makes things more efficient and coherent.

The kind of leadership that I describe in this book, however, doesn't merely improve existing systems a bit by connecting things together. Leaders who work in the middle areas of school districts or networks shouldn't act just as linkages in the transmission systems of educational organizations. They should drive transformational change in their own rights.

This book, like most of my books on teaching, learning, leadership, and change over the past decade and more, come from collaborative work with educators. Within a framework of shared values, my colleagues and I who work together in the academy follow what people in schools and school districts are concerned about and interested in. Our role is to help make sense of what we see and hear, feed it back, and use it to affirm, challenge, and stretch what educators are doing together within a trusted and collaborative relationship of critical friendship. In this respect, *Leading From the Middle* isn't my concept. It was invented by educators we were working with in Ontario as far back as 2009. Our job was to get to grips with what it meant, help to deepen it, and then communicate it to others, including through this book.

My work in Ontario spans two periods of collaborative research and development with ten out of Ontario's more than 70 school districts. The projects were funded by the Council of Directors of Education of Ontario (CODE). Ontario directors are the equivalent of US school district superintendents. In the first period, from 2009 to 2012, my Boston College colleague, Henry Braun, and I were asked to do a retrospective study of how these districts, as a subset of all the districts, had worked together to lead the province's inclusion strategy.[3] We undertook case studies of all ten districts, collected survey data from teachers and principals in all but one of them, and worked collaboratively with district teams in several two-day sessions held in the Greater Toronto area. As former Vice President of Research for US Education Testing Services, Henry did not want to get involved in a book that was not in his field of scholarship, despite all my efforts to persuade him, but he brought unshakeable quantitative rigour to our work, and showed charming humility in joining with the rest of us to undertake qualitative case studies together for the first time in his long career. I will never forget his gracious interjection as a master of the quantitative tradition, when we were all deep into analysis of our data, "Wow, this qualitative research is really hard, isn't it?", he said.

The Ontario districts were varied in socioeconomic composition, geographical location, urban or rural identity, and status as Public, Catholic, and French Language. More details of the study are published in peer-reviewed journals.[4] Our project benefited from the engagement and support of our graduate student team: Lauren Chapman, Maureen Hughes, Karen Lam, Beth Morgan, Kathryn Sallis, Adam Steiner, Matt Welch, and Yu Jin.

The second project was conducted in collaboration with my colleague and close friend, Dennis Shirley, with whom I have written several books deriving from our research and development work together. It took place from 2014 to 2018 in a policy climate that had shifted from an emphasis on improving literacy and mathematics achievement to promoting equity through inclusion and well-being. With one exception, the ten districts in this study were identical to those in the previous one. Graduate student research support was provided by a diverse team comprising Chris Chang Bacon, Mark D'Angelo, and Shanee Washington-Wangia – all of whom now hold positions in US universities.[5] Dennis has elected not to be coauthor of this book, but he has made an enormous contribution to its contents and has provided extensive and valuable feedback on drafts of the final text. I am grateful also to my co-editor of the series in which this book appears, Pak Tee Ng, from the National Institute of Education in Singapore for his thorough feedback.

None of this work would ever have even begun without the support, leadership, and driving passions of three so-called retired Ontario directors and superintendents (equivalent to US school district assistant superintendents), Michelle Forge, John Fauteux, and Michael O'Keefe. This book is one result of their immense leadership legacy. My work in Ontario has also been informed by the privilege I had to be appointed as education advisor to Ontario Premier Kathleen Wynne alongside fellow advisers Carol Campbell, Jean Clinton, Michael Fullan, Carl Grant, and Diane Longboat from 2014 to 2018.

At various points, I also draw on other policy experiences with system-level change. These include working with Beatriz Pont and David Istance at the Organisation for Economic Co-operation and Development (OECD). They invited me to be one of two experts undertaking reviews with them on improving schools, leadership, or assessment, in Finland, Scotland, Wales, and Ireland, respectively.[6] Since 2016, I have also served as one of ten advisers to First Minister Nicola Sturgeon of Scotland where I have learned a lot about changing and making policy rather than just studying it. Together, we have set about turning *Leading From the Middle* into action under political leadership that has been unswervingly committed to equity, inclusion, and human rights for all young people. The research and leadership work of Mel Ainscow, now at the University of Glasgow, helped me understand the importance of cross-district collaboration in England, especially in the Greater Manchester Challenge, and part of Chapter 4 draws on an article we wrote together that first launched *Leading From the Middle* into the education field.[7]

The chapter on Leading Networks From the Middle draws on collaborative development work and reflective writing with Danette Parsley between 2012 and 2019. Danette was a leader at the time for the Northwest Comprehensive Center based in Oregon and asked Dennis Shirley and me to help them design and develop a network that ultimately followed educators' concerns with improving students' engagement in isolated rural schools. Our research team comprised, at different points, Elizabeth Cox, Michael O'Connor, and Minjung Kim.[8] We also enjoyed collaborating with other members of Danette's team, especially Mike Siebersma and Matthew Eide. Project publications are listed at the end of the book.

At the close of Chapter 6, I describe how my University of Ottawa colleagues and I have been turning many of the ideas of Leading Networks Through the Middle into practice in a LEGO Foundation funded project to create a network of schools using play-based learning across Canada. The project has been funded with C$2.7 million over 18 months. My faculty colleagues who have given their time and expertise to this project with unbounded generosity include my co-investigator, Trista Hollweck and, in alphabetical order, Professors Amal Boultif, Megan Cotnam-Kappel, Phyllis Dalley, Michelle Hagerman, Joel Westheimer and Jess Whitley. Graphics are produced by the project team.[9] The design elements of the network were created with Trista Hollweck and further developed with the team. This team includes project managers Josee Lebel and Brigitte Daigle, and over a dozen graduate assistants. Without their tireless efforts, none of the work of the faculty would have been possible. The LEGO Foundation has been a generous and genuine supporter of this work. Special thanks go to Stuart MacAlpine and Tanvi Sethi who have helped us steer this project along. Last, but not least, are teams of educators in the 29 English language and 12 French language schools in seven provinces who value play-based learning for marginalized students in the middle years and have committed themselves to sharing and deepening their work with us and each other.

Towards the close of the book, I describe a global social movement of *Leadership From the Middle* which is the ARC Education Collaboratory. Co-founded with my Norwegian colleague, Dr Yngve Lindvig, this group of seven systems, their ministers, senior officials, and professional leaders, strives to support and spread humanitarian goals in public education within and beyond members' own systems.[10] ARC has benefited and continues to benefit from the collaborative support of Tore Skandsen and his company, IMTEC – the first organization in the world to advance the idea of educational change in the 1970s. Steve Munby has brought his considerable senior leadership experience to working as a superb facilitator for the group, and Trista Hollweck, as the Director of the Collaboratory, steers and also co-facilitates the work and relationships that keep the movement heading in the right direction. The participant systems vary from year to year, depending on administrative and political turnover, but ARC could never exist without the investment of founding or long-standing systems and their leaders who (in alphabetical order) currently are Iceland, Ireland, Nova Scotia, Saskatchewan, Scotland, Uruguay, and Wales.

As this writing process was reaching its closing chapters during the COVID-19 pandemic, I was fortunate to engage closely with the work of two colleagues who have assumed great importance in relation to the book's final arguments. The first was my old friend and colleague, UK Professor David Hargreaves. David and I had communicated on and off over the years since we worked together at Oxford University in the 1980s. But during COVID-19, we resumed a relationship characterized by great intellectual intensity as we shared memoirs, reflections, and eventually, a copy of his remarkably original 2019 book, *Beyond Schooling*.[11] This book and the long conversations we had on email surrounding it, had a significant influence on the structure and direction of this book's closing chapter. Around the same time, I was also asked to contribute to a special issue of a journal celebrating the life and work of University of Minnesota Professor Karen Seashore Louis.[12] This reconnected me with her foundational work on knowledge utilization and high school innovation. The results of that engagement also appear in the final chapter.

My family has contributed more to this book than the usual qualities of personal support that rightly appear in so many other acknowledgements. During COVID-19, my wife, Pauline, who spent her career teaching children in practically every grade and then working as a school administrator in three countries, continuously supervised three of our grandchildren's online learning engagements and helped them survive and thrive during what was a life-shaping experience for them and their generation. I was able to see and support some of that myself and from her, and my three remarkable grandchildren in Ottawa – Jackson and his twin sisters, Amelia and Penelope – I learned a great deal about children's learning and well-being in an up-close and intensely meaningful way. A fourth grandchild, Josephine, added joy to our lives when she was finally able to visit us from Hong Kong at four years old when COVID-19 restrictions there relaxed, and by the time this book went to press, we saw our two-year-old grandson Alec, there, for the very first time. All of them remind me why these seemingly big picture ideas about leadership and change ultimately matter for real children everywhere in our schools.

The book is organized into seven chapters and an epilogue. In the opening chapter, I examine the state of the world we are in, and the wrong ways in which a lot of leadership is responding to it. We are part of that world. It affects us all, especially our students. We must lead everyone in a way where they can understand it, cope with it, and respond to it with full engagement. What we don't want, I argue, is self-absorbed bad leadership that bullies and divides people. Neither do we want technocratic leadership that reduces the significant problems we face to numerical achievement gaps. Nor do we need laissez-faire leadership that leaves schools at the mercy of market forces of individual school competition and all the inequities and fragmentation that result from it. Instead, we need leadership that can regard obstacles as opportunities – including leadership itself. In the systems that responded best to COVID-19, I show, collaborative leadership created the greatest agility and professional unity by assembling everyone who was involved in and affected by the pandemic. These people were not above the crisis, but right in the middle of it together.

Chapter 2 sets out the overall mindset that is required when dealing with a world and its schools that seem to be in constant turmoil. This kind of leadership, I argue, needs to be honestly imperfect, not have all the answers, and depend on others as well as oneself. It is leadership that needs to be non-binary – not Left or Right, progressive or traditional, playful or serious, but able to unite opposites and move beyond them in a both/and rather than either/or universe. Leadership for these times particularly needs to address three paradoxes – to be both top-down and bottom-up; support incremental as well as transformational change; and reconcile professional autonomy with openness and transparency.

Chapter 3 is about addressing these paradoxes by meeting in the middle. This points to a body of policy literature and strategy that advocates for leadership *in*, not *from* the middle as something that connects things, joins them up, and adds another layer, level, or tier of roles and responsibilities between the top and bottom of a system. It looks at an existing middle of school district support and control that has sagged. This is because elected representatives are in increasingly scarce supply, because more sophisticated expertise is needed when issues become more and more complex, and because culture wars are turning old efforts at consensus into rancorous divisions and disputes. The chapter also looks at deliberate attempts to hollow out the middle of school districts because local democracies can get in the way of top-down control, and because they impede the opportunities for private interests to establish more market-based models of schooling. Consequently, any attempt to reconstruct some sort of middle through regional administration or networked relationships in these circumstances tends to focus on linking the top and bottom, whatever ideological orientation it happens to adopt, to get things to run more smoothly, and to increase central government and market control.

From Chapter 4 onwards, we get to the heart of the book: *Leading From the Middle*. Chapter 4 draws on the work of my Boston College colleagues and myself in ten Ontario school districts which invented the concept of *Leading From the Middle*. The middle here is not a linkage but a driving force, a mover and shaker of policy and change towards more inclusive educational values. Indeed, it's even more than that. It is the heart, core and soul of leadership and improvement that transforms inclusion in schools by creating a way for districts to work together collaboratively while respecting the unique forms of diversity that each one of them serves. *Leading From the Middle* (or *Leadership From the Middle*, as I call it, to avoid confusion with a business title that has subsequently emerged in the field), it concludes, requires three things: a *philosophy* of inclusion that inspires everyone; a *culture* of norms, beliefs, and habits, that guides them; and a *structure* of time, space, roles, and responsibilities that supports them.

Chapter 5 compares what the Ontario example can teach us about *Leadership From the Middle* with the discussion in Chapter 4 of increasingly popular policy approaches to developing *Leading In the Middle*. *Leadership From the Middle*, it argues, is not just another strategy. It is a completely different way of thinking about what we mean by the middle, and about policy, change, and education in general. This calls for new metaphors of educational and political change that are less mechanical, and more organic and sustainable in nature. It is why we must think about the middle not as a level or a lever, but as the beating heart of everything we are trying to accomplish together. The chapter discusses the relationship of this newly conceived middle to other parts of the body politic in educational change and then reviews examples where this way of thinking about educational leadership in whole systems is having positive effects.

Chapter 6 looks at *Leadership From the Middle* through networks. It examines *improvement networks* where strong schools and leaders help struggling partners, and *innovation networks* that circulate new knowledge and practices. These insights are based on my experience of co-designing and evaluating networks in Canada, the United States, the United Kingdom, and Australia. The chapter sets out six principles of network design based on reflections on these experiences and on the relevant research on networks.

Chapter 7 addresses three different ways of constructing *Leadership From the Middle* within whole systems and examines the merits and drawbacks of each. These are trust-based systems, self-improving school systems, and social movements.

In the Epilogue, the book closes with some recommendations and guidelines for leaders who find themselves in a position to stimulate and support more and better *Leadership From the Middle*, wherever they happen to be themselves.

That's the run sheet for the book. Now let's begin by looking at the world that everyone is teaching, learning, and leading in. And what a world it is!

1

Looking for Our Leaders

The Big Five

We're in a crisis like we've never seen before; what some are calling an omni-crisis. It feels all pervasive and never-ending. Five huge beasts are breathing down our necks. They're coming for us and our children. We can't run. We can't hide. We're in the fight of our lives. It's time for leaders in education and elsewhere to face up to this Big Five, in our society, and in our schools.

COVID-19 has claimed over five million deaths.[1]
It took over 1.6 billion children out of school.[2] In 2018, the World Health Organization warned that climate change, deforestation, and greater proximity of exotic species to human populations will visit more of these pandemics upon us.[3] Disruption is here for the foreseeable future. We will need to know how to educate our children within and outside a pandemic with equal effectiveness. Our schools and school systems can no longer be lumbering bureaucracies or libertarian free-for-alls. They will need to be incredibly more agile and far more flexible. They will also need to be more coherent and cohesive at the same time. Who can lead them this way?

Climate change is creating catastrophic weather events.
Searing heat, out-of-control wild-fires, raging storms, and devastating floods – these climate-related disruptions and the damage they inflict on schools and communities are adding to the urgent need for ever more agility. But there is even more at stake for children's education

DOI: 10.4324/9781315682921-1

1

than interrupted access. Economic excess has been eating up the planet that feeds it. The next generation is starting to fear it might be the last generation. In a worldwide survey of 10,000 young people in ten countries, 77 per cent agreed with the statement "the future is frightening".[4] Four out of ten were hesitant to have children of their own. How can we rethink an educational system so that it connects people to their natural environment, takes science seriously, and helps young people develop the knowledge and character that will enable and empower them to shape their future?

Wars and rumours of wars are defining our times.
In a 2019 Red Cross survey of 16,000 millennials in 16 countries, 54 per cent agreed that a nuclear war is likely within a decade, 47 per cent thought a Third World War was likely in their lifetimes, and 20 per cent viewed armed conflict as one of the top issues facing the world today.[5] How do we talk to young people about war in ways that are both honest and developmentally appropriate? How do we prepare them to commit to peace in the playground and beyond? How can we bring social studies and the humanities back into the centre of students' learning after decades of being exiled to the curriculum periphery?

One of the consequences of war is also the creation and movement of millions of refugees across the world. In Ukraine, Syria, Afghanistan, and elsewhere, war has robbed children of their education, burdened them with years of post-traumatic stress, deprived them of food, shelter, and other necessities, and sent their families in search of hope and safety across the world.

How do we help young people from war-torn countries deal with the traumas that affect their well-being whether they remain in their home countries, have been placed in refugee camps, or have become newcomers to countries and their schools elsewhere? How do host countries welcome refugees into their midst and be responsive to the cultures and ways of learning that these refugees and other immigrants bring with them? War is not something out there, beyond our schools and influence. It impacts everything that schools do, almost everywhere.

Racism is on the rise.
More and more regions of the world are becoming uninhabitable, leading to contests for water, food, and shelter. An old African

proverb reminds us that "as the waterhole shrinks, the animals look at each other differently". Walls erected on borders, forced deportations, and stoked-up fears that immigrant populations will overwhelm or "replace" the hosts in receiving countries – these spectres of racism and xenophobia haunt us all. We can't delude ourselves anymore that educational equity is mainly a technical matter of closing measured achievement gaps in student test scores. Young people can't feel included or successful if their backgrounds and identities are not recognized and responded to with dignity and integrity in their schools.

But how can schools be responsive to very different kinds of diversity within very different communities? How can they build common cause across many diverse identities of race, social class, gender identity, and disability? How can school curricula reconcile the quest to develop senses of common national pride and heritage with honest confrontations with the stained historical legacies of slavery, colonization, and the oppression of indigenous peoples? How do schools help young people face their history and, in doing so, also face one another and themselves?[6]

Democracy is in peril.

All over the world, populism has been running amok. The Economist Intelligence Unit claims that barely more than 8 per cent of the world's population now live in "full democracies".[7] Attacks on voting rights, refusals to accept election results, and plots to overthrow properly elected governments have been challenging democracies from Canada and the United States to countries in eastern Europe and Latin America. Democracy can no longer be taken for granted.

Young people are easy prey for strong demagogues pedalling simple solutions to complex problems. Although, as we have seen, young people are rightly aware of and concerned about the threats posed by war, climate change, and other crises, a 2022 survey in the United Kingdom found that over 60 per cent of 18–34-year-olds favour having a strong leader who doesn't have to care about elections.[8] In the euphoric rush by the United Nations and others to include and empower more students' voices in educational decision-making, it is dangerous to accept all those voices as they already are.[9] Not every young person is the next Greta Thunberg waiting to happen. Democracy is not the natural or automatic inclination of all or even most young people. It is something that must be developed deliberately. It cannot be left to emerge or evolve by itself.

What can we do to ensure that all students can contribute positively to the life of the school? What can they bring and build rather than just accept and receive? How do we help students to analyse and interpret the news in a discerning way? How do we teach values and responsibility and model this in our schools and education systems? How do we practice greater democracy in our own education systems through devolution of power and decision-making locally, in our schools, and among teachers, students, and families? How do we genuinely empower districts, schools, teachers, and students to give them a sense of agency, autonomy, and responsibility without this leading to chaos, inefficient practice, or the lowering of standards?

How do we help our students distinguish truth from lies and be wary of digital algorithms that reinforce their prejudices and not just their preferences? How can young people experience democracy within their schools and communities, in *how* they learn to live together, as well as *what* they learn about the operation of democracy in political life? How do educational leaders share and distribute leadership not only among and with teachers and other professionals, but also with young people, their parents, and the communities that surround them? In other words, how do leaders enable their schools to be the living and breathing democracies that their societies should also be?

How Are Leaders Responding?

Our world has fallen off its axis. What are our schools and their leaders doing in response? Three major directions are evident, but they are all ill-suited to the nature and scale of these problems. A fourth alternative that I have studied, seen, and advised systems to develop, is the focus of this book. Here's an orientation to the first three.

1. Technical Top-Down Leadership: Rectifying Learning Loss

One argument is that during and after pandemics, wars, and other major disruptions, we should deal with learning loss. After months or even years of interrupted schooling, it's claimed, many students fall behind in literacy and mathematics skills. So, government-imposed, standardized tests are recommended to determine who these students are so we can provide extra time and coaching to close the gaps.10

Contributors to the Royal Society of Canada's report on *COVID-19 and Schools*, however, say this argument is flawed: based on narrow, misleading, and outdated conceptions of achievement.[11] During pandemics, conflicts, displacement of refugees, and other disruptions, where learning moves online, or when it comes to a full stop, young people switch off, tune out, or walk away from learning altogether. They lose the habits of learning and of being motivated and invested in learning. They become disengaged.[12]

Using the testing industry to measure learning loss will steer attention and resources away from a more engaging curriculum that's needed to take on the Big Five. Students need to get re-engaged with their learning, their lives, and the world around them. Large-scale, standardized tests, my own research shows, diminish student engagement, heighten children's anxiety levels, and lead schools to avoid innovation in the grades that are tested.[13] More test preparation and catch-up on basics will almost certainly increase disengagement even more. We need to build young people's knowledge and skills through engaging and important work, not with catch-up exercises and test-prep.

2. Markets and Privatization: Expanding Digital Learning

Had the pandemic hit 20 years earlier, children and schools would have been completely lost. Without digital resources such as learning platforms, Teams, or Zoom, a lot of children's and young people's learning would have screeched to a halt. But the drawbacks of digital learning were also plain for everyone to see – screen-time that far exceeded the limits recommended by national paediatric associations, loss of in-person relationships, difficulties of maintaining motivation, and the sacrifice of green-time outside for screen-time indoors.[14]

Schools mustn't overdo their digital learning commitments now everyone is back. Homework, work folders, messages to parents, assignments, and teacher feedback – do these *all* need to be stored in Google Classroom, and on Chromebooks or other devices? Do we turn too quickly to technology to manage groupwork or split grades when research is telling us that reading and writing online, for most of the time, leads to lower levels of achievement in these essential skills?[15] Digital learning and digital management of learning are not the answer to everything in our schools.

Of course, in moderation, screen-time can help us fend off the Big Five. Climate change scenarios can be simulated and explored with Minecraft and other digital tools. Information about the global fate of democracy can be accessed online from news sources in many parts of the world. Children can expand their experience of diversity by networking virtually with communities elsewhere. Many students with special needs can access and express their learning more effectively by using digital technologies. The results of outdoor field studies in science can be posted on global databases.

But moderation is being overtaken by exuberance and excess. All over the world, teachers' newly enhanced proficiency with digital technologies is fuelling aggressive, private sector marketing of platforms, tools, and devices to public systems at the expense of other tools and approaches that engage students with nature, build belonging, enhance reading for pleasure, and develop well-being, for example. Every school, therefore, should have an ethical technology strategy that manages risks such as digital addiction, excess screen-time, visual-image enhancement by adolescent girls, algorithms that reinforce biases and prejudices, and displacement of other activities like conversation or playing in nature.[16] Students should participate in and sometimes lead these efforts to secure ethical integrity.

3. Bad Leadership: Fomenting Distrust and Resentment

The second decade of the twenty-first century witnessed a lot of what Harvard University professor, Barbara Kellerman, has called *bad leadership*.[17] Bad leadership, Kellerman argues, has at least one of two characteristics. It is unethical, ineffective, or both. Bad leadership is either wrong in its means or its ends, or weak in how it pursues these ends.

In psychiatric terms, many unethical bad leaders are what Manuel Kets De Vries identifies as narcissists, sociopaths, and control-freaks of organizational change.[18] Unethical bad leaders are callous, corrupt, and evil. They oppress their people to advance their own interests. Like Niccolo Machiavelli, they think all leaders should exercise just a little bit of cruelty. They care neither for a noble cause, nor for the people who serve and follow them. They are the Pol Pots of genocide, the Lady Macbeths of fiction, and the Alexander the Greats of history (Alexander even tortured his own children just for the fun of it!). Unethical bad leaders are Frank and Claire Underwood in *House of Cards* rather than Leo Bartlett in *The West Wing*.

Bad leaders can be strong leaders – people with inexhaustible energy, steely determination and an iron will. Researchers who advance seemingly neutral frameworks supporting "strong leadership" therefore need to be cautious.[19] Strong leadership can be evil as well as effective. It can suddenly become *strongman l*eadership.[20] The manifestation of strong leadership as a set of narcissistic vices rather than selfless virtues is most obvious in the behaviour of political demagogues who stoke up division and resentment to advance their own interests.

Like Narcissus himself, narcissists love to look at their own reflection. The American Psychiatric Association has categorized narcissism as a personality disorder: "an all-pervasive pattern of grandiosity, need for admiration or adulation and lack of empathy".[21]

Narcissistic leaders are "driven by grandiose fantasies about themselves".[22] "Pathological narcissists are selfish and inconsiderate, demand excessive attention, feel entitled, and pursue power and prestige at all costs."[23]

How do narcissistic leaders survive with personalities like this? What's in it for their followers? Amid inequity and alienation, when followers feel abandoned and lost, narcissistic leaders offer them acknowledgement, hope, and a sense of direction. The dangerous attraction of gurus, as the psychiatrist Anthony Storr once wrote, is that they "awaken the child that is latent in us all".[24]

Explained appropriately, the narrative of totalitarian populism can be understood by almost any age group. One example is the 2022 animated movie, *The Sea Beast*.[25] The movie's plot concerns a monarchy that buttresses its power with a fake history about a demonized enemy of predatory sea beasts that people are incited to try and slay to protect themselves. By focusing on this manufactured external threat, the king and queen deflect attention from the injustices and inequities that benefit their own elite.

In the politics of education, narcissistic leaders rouse up enmity to turn people against each other and enlarge their own ego. Narcissistic leaders have resisted initiatives to teach the science of climate change and have proposed that creationism should stand on an equal footing with the evidence of evolution. They have expressed outrage about the installation of gender-neutral bathrooms in schools, even though gender neutrality has characterized aircraft bathrooms for decades. Narcissistic leaders declare wars on *woke* which has become a term of abuse even though the concept was initially introduced by African Americans to address problems of racism and challenges of establishing social justice.[26] They insist that success is unaffected by race, ethnicity, or institutionalized privilege and comes from ability, effort, and self-discipline alone. Unethical bad leaders foment moral panics about alleged efforts to spin national cultures and histories negatively by imposing burdens of psychological guilt on white children. Unethical bad leaders have also conducted purges of well-regarded books that include non-traditional families, or that use graphic text forms to narrate historical events like the Holocaust, for example.[27]

Summary

Growing up in the twenty-first century must sometimes feel like being dragged through an utterly chaotic period of war, famine, and pestilence by modern-day horsemen of the apocalypse. But there are other ways for leaders in education and society to respond to these omni-crises than in the three all-too-common forms I have described here.

We needn't tighten our grip on control by reducing everything to technical problems such as measured learning losses and achievement gaps that bolster the interests of testing companies but do little to restore young people's engagement with learning or with their quality of life.

We mustn't hand over everything to market forces and corporate interests which oversell and overclaim how digital and other technologies will resolve all our problems for us, in learning and in life.

Finally, the overconfident and overbearing approaches of unethical bad leadership must not be allowed to proclaim false certainties that pit the strong against the weak, and the privileged against the marginalized, as resources start to disappear, and opportunities begin to shrink.

These are not the best ways or the right ways for our leaders to overcome the formidable obstacles that are standing in the way of progress. There is another proven and practical alternative that can get past these obstacles in ways that will benefit everyone, not just a privileged few. One of the things that characterizes this alternative is that it doesn't always regard obstacles as being in the way of our aspirations and ambitions. Obstacles, rather, are often the way forward, in and of themselves

The Obstacle *Is* the Way

In his bestselling book, *The Obstacle Is the Way*, Ryan Holiday begins by quoting the wise words of Roman Emperor Marcus Aurelius. If we accommodate and adapt, Emperor Aurelius declared, we will find that "the impediment to action advances action. What stands in the way becomes the way".[28] Holiday's book is full of examples of this principle in operation. We've all experienced obstacles in our work. Who among us hasn't had a promotion we didn't get, a boss we couldn't stand, a proposal that was rejected, or circumstances like a recession or a pandemic that took the bottom out of our world and seemed to destroy everything we had been striving for?

What Holiday asks us to do is to treat these obstacles as opportunities. When we've been blocked, opposed, rejected, or just defeated by unexpected twists of circumstance, how do we react? That, says Holiday, is the key question. He outlines dispositions that can help us to deal with formidable obstacles. Stay calm. Be objective. Try to look at the obstacle differently. Be wilful and persistent. Explore unconventional approaches. Don't withdraw or hesitate but be ready to act and move forward. Holiday might also have added: don't do all this by yourself but find others who can get past the obstacle with you.

Three highly accomplished colleagues and friends of mine all faced incredible obstacles in their childhood that eventually became their pathways to stunning success.

The first is the late *Sir Ken Robinson*. A giant in the field of creativity, and winner of the 2011 LEGO Prize for contributions to the lives of children, Sir Ken is best known for delivering the most downloaded TED Talk of all time, attracting upwards of 73 million views.[29] Sir Ken was raised in modest circumstances in Liverpool, England, at the time The Beatles were just starting out in The Cavern Club. He might have become a professional football player for Everton Football Club, like his brother Neil, but at the age of four, he contracted polio. The archive that is being curated of his work and life includes the metal callipers that had to be placed on his legs just so he could walk. Indeed, Sir Ken had a pronounced limp for the rest of his life. As he often recalled, though, this physical disability was also a gift. It led him to channel his energies into the arts, creative thinking, and education. Ultimately, he became one of the most sought-after speakers and advisers on education, creativity, and the arts in the world.

Seymour B. Sarason, who lived into his 90s, is a second person whose obstacles in early life became his way. Sarason wrote *The Culture of the School and the Problem of Change* in 1971.[30] It was, arguably, the first work to establish educational change as a field of action and study. Born in 1919, in Brooklyn, New York, Sarason was the son of Jewish immigrant parents. In his autobiography, one of more than 30 books that he authored, Sarason reflects on his lifelong feelings of being an outsider.[31] In addition to his struggle to establish himself academically at a time of rampant antisemitism in higher education, Sarason (like Robinson) also contracted polio early in life and had to have his upper body encased in a brace or a cast when he was in high school. The legacy of Sarason's disability which, as a young man, marked him out in a community where his peers had gone to fight in the Second World War, had a direct bearing on his early career interest in people who had other disabilities – ones of what was then called mental retardation or handicap. This inspired him, in turn, to establish the field of community psychology. Paradoxically, this ambitious outsider and prominent advocate for other underdogs owed much of his success to the double marginalization of his childhood upbringing and disability; to the obstacles that became his way.

Harvard University professor, Howard Gardner, the famed creator of the theory of multiple intelligences, is a third person whose obstacles became his way. Gardner's parents narrowly escaped the Holocaust when they arrived as immigrants to the United States, on Kristallnacht, in November 1938.[32] This was an infamous night when synagogues, stores, and other buildings were ransacked by German paramilitary forces. When Howard was still in his mother's womb, his older brother perished in a sledding accident. As a result, his parents kept him from engaging in sports and other strenuous activities. Indeed, they later told him, after the traumas of fleeing from the Nazis, settling in another country, and losing their first-born child, his mother's pregnancy with Howard was the only thing that prevented her and her husband from committing suicide. Barred from physical engagements and burdened with this awesome responsibility, Gardner channelled his energies into a life of the mind. This culminated in him becoming one of the world's leading authorities in cognitive psychology. The obstacle to his possible accomplishment in one area became the gateway to his stellar achievements in another.

I read Holiday's book during a return to the UK, to collect an honorary doctorate from the University of Bolton, the closest university to my hometown. In celebration of or perhaps as a kind of pilgrimage to mark this occasion, I invited a friend of mine from the university, David Hopkins, to hike 13 miles across bleak moorlands with me from Bolton to my first home. Even in the best circumstances, the land is wild and often featureless. But the COVID-19 pandemic had made it even worse.

In several places, our pathway had fallen into complete disuse. Eventually, it led us into a wood, on a narrow way flanked by high barbed wire fences. Storms had blown down many trees that now blocked our route. We got over the first tree trunk and crawled under a second. But then, an enormous monster of a tree, a mass of tangled and seemingly impenetrable limbs, had fallen in front of us. There seemed to be no way over, under, around, or through it. Then I recalled Holiday's book. How, I asked myself, might this obstacle be my way? I looked at the limbs and branches. They lay slightly slanted on a sideways and upward incline between the fences. I went to one end, mounted a fallen limb, clung onto one above it, then undertook an arboreal traverse from one side to the other. It was precarious, but it did indeed become the way as I eventually reached the other end and was able to slide back down to the ground on the far side. I had worked with the tree rather than battled against it. Our obstacle had become our way.

Unexpected Opportunities

It's easy for the Big Five omni-crisis of multiple and never-ending challenges to make us feel hopeless and helpless. But it also offers breakthroughs and opportunities that did not exist, or that we could not see before. Because of the crisis, rather than despite it, we can now see some new ways forward to achieve important goals in and through education.

Restoring Learning for a Purpose

For more than two decades, the mounting debts incurred by pursuing a college degree turned more and more students towards studying business and law for purely utilitarian reasons so that they could secure careers that would offer them financial security and prosperity.[33] Money became their driver, more than the moral purpose of the contribution they might make to society. But after all the machinations that led to Britain's exit (Brexit) from Europe, applications to study political science for an undergraduate degree in parts of the United Kingdom increased.[34] Meanwhile, in the United States, after Donald Trump's accession to the US presidency and following repeated challenges by him and his associates to election processes and results, constitutional law moved from being one of the dullest specializations of a US law degree, to becoming one of its most sought-after options.[35] And in my own university in Ottawa, like in many others, the COVID-19 pandemic turned epidemiology from being a peripheral area of scientific study into one of the most popular specializations in higher education. Social purpose has returned as one of the biggest reasons for studying for a higher education degree.

Re-inventing Technical and Vocational Learning

The COVID-19 pandemic, the war in Ukraine and even anti-vaccine protests on the US–Canadian border have severely disrupted global supply chains in manufacturing and food supply at different times.[36] The complacent assumption that we could produce anything, anywhere, at the cheapest cost and distribute it effortlessly to its market destinations in a world without meaningful borders has been turned upside down. The links in global supply chains are no longer secure. So, nation after nation is moving at least some parts of manufacturing and agricultural production closer to home.[37] This is bringing vocational education and the creation of high skill and high wage economies rather than ones based on finance and services alone, back to the forefront of many nations' educational policy priorities.[38] Vocational education for high status jobs bestowing craft pride on those who perform them addresses the purposes of students who want dignified, valued, and skilled jobs but don't necessarily want to take traditional college academic programmes. It's a chance to give the Cinderella subject of vocational education the pride of place that it has long enjoyed in high-skill economies such as Germany's.

Rethinking High-Stakes Assessments

In almost every country, as young people were sent home from school during the COVID-19 pandemic until it was medically safe to return, tests that measured student performance, and examinations that determined young people's future career paths, were suspended for up to two years. Tests that had been regarded as indispensable for accountability and examination purposes were suddenly jettisoned. As systems developed alternative ways of assessing what their students knew and were able to do, the testing and exam hiatus unleashed widespread protests as to whether they should ever come back in their conventional form. In Ireland, for example, I was part of a review of aspects of its assessment and grading processes during COVID-19. The country's long-standing sit-down school leaving certificate has determined 100 per cent of everyone's future. It is a matter of public record that the exam creates immense stress, narrows the curriculum, and has led to a proliferation of "grind schools" that unfairly favour the students of economically privileged parents.[39] Following the review process, Ireland's education minister announced that, in the future, the leaving examination would eventually be responsible for no more than 60 per cent rather than 100 per cent of young people's final grades, and that complementary teacher-based assessments would be developed to judge young people's achievements.[40]

Summary

Crises, it is sometimes said, shouldn't be wasted. Problems can turn out to be our friends. Because of COVID-19 and the inescapable impact of the Big Five omni-crisis, young people are choosing careers and courses of study that are about facing the future and affecting it, rather than hiding away from it or concentrating only on themselves. Vocational education is making a long overdue comeback. And the tests and exams that no one thought could ever be changed are being dialled back all over the world. These are just three examples of how obstacles have turned into pathways.

There are others. Teachers almost everywhere had to acquire and improve their skills in digital technologies in a matter of days and have become both more competent and more critical users of screen-based learning as a result. The need to keep down infection rates among children during the COVID-19 pandemic moved more learning outdoors, which has led, in turn, to subsequent increases in outdoor learning and to the creation of more outdoor learning spaces.[41] The conventional wisdom has been that educational change can only be gradual, as educators needed time to adapt to it. But when everyone has a sense of common urgency, change, we now know, can be incredibly fast. This also applies to leadership.

Overcoming Leadership Obstacles

One of the greatest obstacles for educational leaders during COVID-19 was the sheer lack of certainty about what to do next in an environment where new problems emerged, and fresh crises erupted on a weekly basis. Leaders found themselves confronting problems they had never seen before, with few or new precedents to guide them, in areas that were totally outside their knowledge base or skillset. Policy makers who tried to bludgeon their way through these obstacles with top-down edicts and mandates that seemed arbitrary, inconsistent, and even contradictory often made the crisis worse by creating intense anxiety, resentment, and resistance. Some governments' self-serving efforts to manage COVID-19 autocratically cost them dearly in the next elections.

The Canadian province of Alberta, for example, introduced a controversial draft new curriculum right in the middle of the pandemic. In a survey by the Alberta Teachers Association of over 2,500 educators' responses to COVID-19 in May 2021, over 90 per cent of them were moderately or very concerned about the reform. One of them described the political environment as "demoralizing".[42]

Other countries had more success with managing the COVID-19 crisis in education, though. Much of this depended on the collaborative capacity of governments to value and harness educators' professional judgements as part of the decision-making process. Several months into the pandemic, the Organisation for Economic Co-operation and Development (OECD) published a policy review of how countries were managing COVID-19 in education.[43] Many of the most successful systems had established collaborative teams, working groups, or committees, including with teachers' and principals' associations. They then collected and analysed data together, at the highest levels of policy, to determine and lead the response. Instead of seeing local professionals as obstacles to top-down mandates and implementation, the apparent chaos was harnessed to develop solutions from and with those who were closest to the local problems.

One example is Scotland, where I serve on a team of ten education advisers to the government. Scotland established a *COVID-19 Education Recovery Group* (CERG), that met weekly, online, and was chaired by the Minister of Education.[44] There had already been a systematic effort over several years to strengthen collaboration at all levels throughout the Scottish education system. When COVID-19 hit, this prior commitment to collaborative ways of working paid dividends. A report by Education Scotland on the country's management of COVID-19 in education quoted leaders who valued partnerships with trade unions and the National Health Service, and who felt local authorities were really working in strong teams that were close to the ground and able to respond to crises.[45]

Scotland's approach to managing schools during COVID-19 is one example of *Leadership From the Middle* – the focus of this book. The COVID-19 pandemic exposed the ineffectiveness of top-down policy solutions under complex conditions of great uncertainty and rapid change. In Scotland, Ireland, and elsewhere, leaders were afforded a better way to get their educational systems through the omni-crisis; one that involved collaborating with others, in the middle, in an agile and inclusive way.

Leading From the Middle

At this existential tipping point, young people don't need more interminable tests, ideologically driven disruptions, or constant digital distraction. They need to voice their feelings about the future, and advocate for a world that is better, fairer, and more sustainable. They need to think and act collectively, rather than shade in test boxes or stare at screens for hours on end. Young people need to find and fulfil a sense of meaning and purpose in their lives, to be part of the solution to the mess we are in. It will be through meaningful and purposeful work, rather than through catch-up classes that deal with measured learning loss, that members of the coming adult generation will master the knowledge and skills that will make them effective, inspired, and hopeful agents of change.

None of this can be achieved by top-down leadership that is suited, at best, to implementing technical solutions to narrowly defined problems like closing achievement gaps. Complex problems in an omni-crisis world require sophisticated solutions that are inclusive, agile, and responsive. This means rethinking how we do leadership.

2

LEADERSHIP
PARADOXES

Leading Through Complexity

Effective leadership is rarely simple, even though demagogues try to
make it so. In modern societies, in fast-moving organizations, and
in environments facing constant change, leadership is almost never
straightforward. There are few moments when knowing what to do
and how to do it are unambiguous. Required solutions are rarely
obvious and incontrovertible. For instance, what do you do in a pandemic when the scientific evidence is mixed? When should schools be
opened and when should they be closed? How can children's needs
and concerns be reconciled with those of the adults who educate
them? In the middle of an overwhelming crisis, how can you sustain
the lives and health of others without neglecting to sustain yourself?
So much of what leaders must decide does not come down to right
or wrong answers. Leaders are not robots or algorithms. They make
human judgements by dealing with dilemmas, choosing better courses
of action over worse ones, or even selecting less bad solutions compared to truly awful alternatives.

When we promote one person over another who is also qualified
and deserving; when we cannot find budget support for all the worthy
initiatives that people are pursuing; when we cannot always leave our
door open because that would dissolve the boundaries that protect our
own psychological health – in these and so many other cases, leadership is about making hard choices between competing priorities. This
inalienable aspect of leadership doesn't always make the leader the
most popular person around.

DOI: 10.4324/9781315682921-2   17

Imperfect Leadership

One way of responding to leaders' inability to solve every problem is to be stoic and phlegmatic; to accept the limitations of the situation, of the job, and of one's own skills and character. Steve Munby, former CEO of England's national organization that trained and developed all school leaders, turns this sense of pragmatic necessity into a positive philosophy by arguing for what he calls *Imperfect Leadership*.[1] Imperfect leadership, Munby argues, is something to celebrate. It is the opposite of the superhero myth of leaders who try to accomplish everything by themselves. Imperfect leaders "know their own strengths and weaknesses", show empathy for other people and rely on them to round out the necessary skillsets that they don't cover themselves.[2] They are confident, but not arrogant. They apologize for errors and learn from their mistakes. At the end of the day, although they are passionate and relentless about pursuing goals that will benefit and even transform the lives of the people they serve, they are also comfortable in their own skin – warts and all.

In most areas of life, perfection is a futile goal. Zero-tolerance policies, elimination of achievement gaps, insisting that failure is not an option, and unassailable leadership – in most circumstances, these are all unattainable ends. Not only are they unattainable. They are not even desirable. The cosmetically altered wrinkle-free face, the orthodontically perfect row of teeth, the flawlessly scripted TED Talk – don't all these lose a vital part of what makes us human, distinct, and interesting? As the late Leonard Cohen pointed out, "there is crack in everything". That, he added, is "where the light gets in".[3]

Striving for excellence is admirable. Pursuing perfection is a trap. The French writer, Voltaire, put it best when he stated that "The perfect is the enemy of the good."[4] In *Overcoming Perfectionism*, Anne W. Smith argues that "the desire to be superhuman becomes a problem when we begin to believe that perfection is actually possible and even necessary for self-esteem, success, peace of mind, and acceptance by others".[5] Relentless perfectionism, she writes, ultimately leads to obsessiveness, depression, addictive behaviour, and burnout.

Being an imperfect leader is about how we handle our imperfections, and make the most of them, while eliminating or at least mitigating their harmful effects on others. Imperfect leadership is about acknowledging our own and each other's flaws, learning from them, and even loving each other for them a bit – like the brilliant but absent-minded professor, the efficient manager who sometimes gets too uptight, or the passionate yet vulnerable leader whose heart on their sleeve may beat too loudly for other people's comfort.

For Munby, being an imperfect leader means not being driven by either/or thinking, or even by trade-offs to resolve dilemmas. This way of thinking embraces opposites and comes up with both/and rather than either/or solutions that integrate them effectively.

Both/And Leadership

The master of both/and thinking in education was the philosopher John Dewey. Dewey brought together educational alternatives that other people put asunder. Take the opposition between interests and disciplines. Should teachers encourage learners to follow their own interests, or should young people be inducted into disciplines of mind and knowledge? Dewey's answer was that interest and discipline are interconnected rather than opposed to each other. To develop an interest demands "continuity of attention and endurance", he said. Discipline, or "continuous attention", "is its fruit".[6]

Then there is the all-too-common and sometimes hostile ploy to oppose work against play. Should children be able to experience joyful learning through play, or does this detract from and damage serious engagement with disciplined hard work in literacy, mathematics, and foundational knowledge? Dewey insisted that "the defining characteristic of play is not amusement nor aimlessness".[7] At the same time, he said, the importance of work should not be reduced to drudgery, that, like in the worst factories, reduces schoolwork to something "inherently repulsive (that is) enduring for the sake of averting something even more repulsive" (punishment) "or of securing a gain hitched on by others".[8] Rather, Dewey stated, as playful activities "grow more complicated" and "gain added meaning by greater attention to specific results" "they pass gradually into work". Instead of play being "idle excitement for the well-to-do" and work being "uncongenial labor for the poor", great work often feels like engrossing play, and mature play soon transitions into hard work.[9]

Munby never quotes Dewey, but he gets Dewey's message. For example, Munby takes two apparent opposites – love and power – and shows how great leaders pay attention to both. He quotes Martin Luther King: "Power without love is reckless and abusive, and love without power is sentimental and anemic."[10] It's important, Munby believes, that leaders use their power, set a demanding pace and be willing to challenge those who are insufficiently bold or determined. At the same time, he continues, leaders should support those whom they challenge and be willing to have others challenge themselves too in relationships of trust and respect. Leaders must use their power to be "strong and proud, who challenge mediocre practice, who drive tirelessly towards improvement, who are determined to make a difference".[11] But leaders must also love their colleagues and community. These must be leaders who "build on the achievements of former teachers and leaders, who are inclusive and engaging, whose egos don't get in the way . . . who are quick to praise others rather than seek it for themselves".[12]

Munby's both/and approach to leadership treats it in many ways as an individual psychological disposition. By contrast, Dewey's stance is somewhat abstract and philosophical. In an imperfect world, we also need both/and strategies in leadership of systems, as well as abstract assertions or individual actions. These strategies frame choices, dilemmas, and tensions as paradoxes.

Leading Through Paradox

A paradox is a seemingly self-contradictory proposition that turns out to be true. One of the best examples of paradoxical thinking in leadership and change management was devised in the 1980s by Kjeld Kirk Kristiansen, the grandson of Ole Kirk Kristiansen – the founder of the iconic global company, LEGO. The LEGO brand has had stellar success, recognition, and profitability. But LEGO has also experienced crises and downturns in its long history. Kristiansen, the grandson, led an approach to LEGO's management that now hangs on the walls of every LEGO manager's office as well as in the company's museum in Billund, Denmark. This approach, that is well-known throughout the management field, is *The 11 Paradoxes of Management* (see Figure 2.1).[13]

THE 11 PARADOXES OF MANAGEMENT

To be able to establish a close relationship to your employees,	– and to keep proper distance
To take the lead,	– and to recede into the background
To show the employee confidence,	– and to be aware of their doings
To be tolerant,	– and to know how you want things done
To be concerned about your own field of responsibility,	– and at the same time to be loyal to the overall goals of the company
To plan your working-day carefully,	– and to be flexible to your planning
To express your opinion,	– and to be diplomatic
To be visionary,	– and to keep both feet firmly on the ground
To aim at consensus,	– and to be able to cut through
To be dynamic,	– but also thoughtful
To be self-confident,	– and humble

Figure 2.1 The 11 Paradoxes of Management

Every leader will be aware of how these paradoxes present difficult choices and dilemmas for them. For example, as an old country and western song almost puts it, it's hard to be humble when you're proud.[14] But somehow leaders must be both of these things. Employees must be trusted, but not blindly. Developing relationships with those you lead is important. But descending into a corrupt organization that does favours for friends must be avoided at all costs. These things are fine lines, and sometimes blurred lines, yet leaders must find a way of walking them.

In 2008, writing in the *Academy of Management Journal*, Lotte Luscher and Marianne Lewis described their efforts to get LEGO managers to apply these iconic principles which, they felt, had not been used enough by them. As a result of their coaching and mentoring support, they reported, LEGO managers were more able to identify and apply both/and options such as leading the way *and* receding into the background, "sharing their knowledge to help employees learn to solve problems themselves".[15] Leading through paradox is not just an abstraction or an ideal, then. It is achievable in practice.

These LEGO paradoxes are largely addressed to individuals. How might they also apply across and beyond such leaders? Singapore educational leadership specialist, Pak Tee Ng, describes how the whole national educational system and wider culture of his country rests on working with paradoxes. In *Learning from Singapore: The Power of Paradoxes*, he sets out what he calls "paradoxes to be appreciated" in the Singapore system. This is a system that believes:

- children will learn more if educators teach less;
- children can develop creativity *and* perform well on standardized tests;
- traditional values can coexist with innovative habits;
- a highly centralized system can still encourage a considerable amount of decentralized responsibility.[16]

In Singaporean culture, paradoxical thinking plays a big part in improvement. As Pak Tee Ng himself points out, although people in Western cultures believe that oil and water don't mix, in Asian cooking they do! This chapter explores three paradoxes of system leadership that face many educational leaders in conditions of complexity:

- Bottom Up and Top Down
- Incremental and Transformational Change
- Autonomy and Transparency

Bottom Up and Top Down

In the mid 1990s, my colleague and friend, Michael Fullan, declared that "neither top-down nor bottom-up strategies for educational reform work. What is required is a more sophisticated blend of the two".[17]

When top-down reform is associated with bad leadership, most educators probably wouldn't want it to work anyway. But not all top-down reform has dubious intent. It may reflect a sincere government effort to implement changes that raise standards or increase equity, for example. Yet, as early as the mid 1990s, Fullan could already point to research on testing and accountability reforms that threw educators into a "crisis mentality" and drove them to leap to solutions too quickly. These solutions, like narrowing the curriculum to raise test scores, harmed the very things they were supposed to improve. They also undermined teacher collaboration and morale. "Governments can't mandate what matters", Fullan concluded, "because what matters most is local motivation, skill, know-how, and commitment".[18]

By the year 2000, Fullan had changed his mind about top-down leadership. Not all of it was bad, it seemed. Shortly after, with the benefit of his role as the Premier of Ontario's education adviser, the province tried to avoid the mistakes of England and the United States, which had raised scores by restricting students' learning to what was easily tested, and by imposing sanctions on schools that didn't improve. Fullan's team established a *guiding coalition* that included professional leaders and other partners focused on a small number of priorities related to literacy, mathematics, and high school graduation rates.[19] Schools were provided with extensive professional development and financial support for implementation. Teachers were given support from mentors and coaches. Poor performing schools weren't punished by closing them down or firing their principals. After several years of top-down reform, literacy attainment improved significantly and sustainably, and achievement gaps narrowed for several groups, including second language learners and children with learning disabilities.[20] The right kind of top-down reform, it seemed, could get positive results.

Ontario's strategy yielded measurable success in educational change goals that were simple and few. Some years later, though, Fullan conceded that top-down strategies are weakly suited to complex and uncertain environments where innovation must be encouraged, and where multiple initiatives are pursued simultaneously.[21] Other initial converts to top-down reform like Harvard University professor, Richard Elmore, also learned that mandated reform was "either very superficial or downright wrong" because it was naïve about the complexity of change.[22]

Top-down change in education can work when the purpose is straightforward, the results are easily measured, and there is public confidence in schools. It is anachronistic, however, when the system's goals are complex. Creativity, critical thinking, inclusion, well-being, and senses of belonging are impossible to implement from the top because leaders cannot possibly know everything across such a broad span of student learning as it affects an increasingly diverse population.

When top-down approaches fail, reformers often go the other way. The pendulum swings. They promote greater autonomy for schools and teachers, increased freedom for curriculum design, and personalized approaches to learning. But the history of bottom-up innovation and school autonomy is not impressive, either. In the 1960s and 1970s, innovative ideas often didn't spread beyond a few isolated classrooms or schools.[23] Even when they did, their implementation was often superficial.[24] Teachers sometimes used new methods that they didn't fully understand.

This does not mean that bottom-up innovations have no value. A system does not have to adopt an idea or strategy across all or most of its schools for an innovation to have widespread impact. Howard Gardner, for example, has never attempted to implement or directly influence any system to implement his ideas wholesale, but in his 2009 book on *Multiple Intelligences Around the World*, 42 authors from 15 countries on five continents write about the numerous ways in which they have applied them.[25]

Although innovative experiments are frequently dismissed for being little more than atypical outliers that disappear when leaders leave, when teachers move on, when resources are withdrawn, or when political support is removed, this does not mean they have no lasting influence or leave no legacy. In a study of change over three decades and more in eight Ontario and US secondary schools, my colleagues and I learned that although the early energy of innovative secondary schools did tend to dissipate over time, founding innovators in these schools carried what they learned with them to other schools, in their next jobs.[26] Indeed, innovative schools could become incubators for new leaders, who would go on to rise through the system, into senior leadership positions, where their transformational ideas about equity, inclusion, cooperative learning, and more helped to shape new educational policies in the future.

Programmes *within* schools, as well as coaching and professional development support *for* schools, often benefit from recruiting educators who have cut their innovative teeth elsewhere. Instead of being outliers, they are more like inlays of innovation. In their study of 30 carefully chosen US high schools, Jal Mehta and Sarah Fine didn't discover the embedded uses of deeper learning that they were hoping to find. But they did unearth innovative practices *within* almost every school.[27] These were in after-school activities, extra-curricular programmes, academic options, and so on. Columbia University professor, Tom Hatch, notes that if these in-school innovative inlays are pulled together coherently, "these micro-developments can accumulate to create new and unanticipated opportunities for systemic improvements in learning on a broad scale" when the time is ripe.[28]

Bottom-up innovations can spread diffusely, and they can turn their acolytes into sleeper cells within traditional systems who bring those systems to life when they assume more power later in their careers.[29] When there are top-down strategies to expand these local innovations in real time and over time, bottom-up change may have better prospects for success than has often been thought.

Fullan was right the first time. On their own, neither top-down nor bottom-up strategies work. But, as we will see, there *are* ways to combine and bring them together. This can happen when leaders at the top define clear senses of direction, inspire their educators to realize a vision, provide valuable resources of time and support, and then create structures and processes for ideas to percolate up from the bottom in tune with the vision and in relationship with each other. If leaders create conditions and directions for change rather than micromanaging the change process, then the top and bottom can come together. They can begin to meet in the middle.

Incremental and Transformational Change

At some point, most organizations must face the fact that they are losing their edge, falling behind their competitors, or failing to keep up with the times. Businesses with declining profits, sports teams with fading reputations, religious organizations that are losing followers, and educational systems that are not improving and seem stuck in a rut are all confronted with a choice on which their continued success and survival may hinge. Should they oil the machine, make it more efficient, and look to make many small and cumulative incremental changes in existing practices? Or should they turn the whole organization upside down and have a complete rethink?

In our 2009 book on *The Fourth Way*, Dennis Shirley and I asked:

> Should schools be improving what they already do, and undertake everything in their power to make it better, and more effective? Or should they be embracing innovation . . . not merely making their existing practice more effective but transforming that practice and perhaps even the nature of their institutions altogether?[30]

More than a decade later, in 2022, Tom Hatch revisited the same question in *The Education We Need for a Future We Can't Predict*. His answer is deceptively simple: "The challenges are so great that we have to do both." "We need to both improve schools and transform education", he says.[31] Incremental school improvement might be the normal run of affairs, but greater transformations can occur when "education systems and the efforts to improve them reflect the social, cultural, geographic, political, and economic conditions in which those improvement efforts take place".[32]

Efforts at undertaking large-scale innovation may not work in cultures like England, Australia, and the United States where inequality is high, social mobility is low, and cultures of individualism and private education are pervasive. But elsewhere, as the examples in Table 2.1 illustrate, when values in society and education are aligned, and when educational change is an integral part of social transformation, then large-scale change is and has been possible.

Systemwide transformations that bring about profound improvements may be difficult in highly competitive and unequal societies

Table 2.1 Three Examples of System Transformation

Iceland	Up to the start of this century, *Iceland* recorded extremely high levels of school dropout along with drug and alcohol abuse among its youth. The government responded by constructing leisure centres that provided after-school activities, free of charge, with qualified sports coaches. The *Huffington Post* noted that "from 1998 to 2016, the percentage of 15 to 16 year old Icelandic youth drunk in the past 30 days declined from 42% to 5%; daily cigarette smoking dropped from 23% to 3%; and having used cannabis one or more times fell from 17% to 5%".[33] From having one of the worst records in the world on student well-being, Iceland now has one of the best.

Estonia	After the collapse of the former Soviet Republic, *Estonia* became a world leader in technology. The country in which Skype was invented took a "Tiger Leap" in 1996 by promoting internet use, moving elections online, sponsoring digital citizenship by crowdsourcing the public's ideas, teaching coding from the age of seven, and making all the curriculum available digitally.[34] This not only enabled Estonia to make a smooth transition to online learning during the COVID-19 pandemic; it also helps explain its positioning as Europe's highest performer on the international PISA results for students aged 15.
Uruguay	In 2007, *Uruguay* became the world's first nation to introduce one laptop per child. It then established a national education agency that creates curriculum materials online –a lifesaver for teachers during the pandemic – and that produces innovative materials and coaching support, with and without technology, to stimulate educational innovation in large numbers of its schools.[35] Its agency, *Plan Ceibal*, and its staff of 500 now advise other systems all over the world about how to innovate successfully across whole systems.

like England and the United States where top-down control prevails and learning goals are easily measured and limited. But their chances of success are more likely where values in society are undergoing profound transformations. A chaotic world where the Big Five are coming after us is provoking considerably more transformational thinking far beyond the examples listed above.

Outside of these transformational moments, Hatch still urges people not to get disconsolate about the difficulty of wholesale improvement. Even in more routine times, he insists, significant changes can still be made by promoting and expanding what he calls "high-leverage" micro-innovations in particular areas of the school's operation. These can lead to "specific, concrete and visible improvements in the schools we have".[36] Hatch includes after-school programmes, one-on-one tutoring support, and expanded learning time among changes that consistently lead to gains in student achievement, attendance, and equity. Positive change doesn't always have to transform everything at once. And even transformation requires a lot of attention to detail so that new practices of teaching are not just joyful but also effective; so that digital technology is used carefully rather than frivolously; and so that student voice is listened to mindfully rather than embraced or dismissed unthinkingly.

What Hatch's book helps us to see is that we shouldn't locate educational reform initiatives or overall performance of a school or a system on a single continuum that extends from "poor" to "proficient" to "good" to "great". The nature and ambition of a school's or system's goals and purposes, their direction of travel, are as important as the progress towards accomplishing them.

As we have started to engage with the omni-crisis that faces us all, educational goals the world over have shifted from being concerned with tested achievement and measured achievement gaps in basic skills of literacy, mathematics, and, to a lesser extent, science, towards broader and bolder educational goals and outcomes. The United Nations' 17 Sustainable Development Goals seek to build more equitable, humane, and sustainable educational systems.[37] The OECD's global competencies set out skillsets such as the ability to "understand and appreciate the perspectives and world views of others", that will create dynamic, flexible, inclusive, and healthy societies through education.[38] And, since 2015, the global network of educational systems that I co-founded and now chair in the ARC Education project, has been promoting the core educational values of broad (not narrow) excellence, equity, inclusion, well-being, democracy, and human rights.[39]

The global shift towards a transformational set of outcomes and processes echoes some very distinguished educational traditions: education that concentrates on the "whole-child" or on development of the whole person in a lifelong-learning process;[40] the project method of the United States in the 1920s;[41] and the "progressive" approach of English primary schools in the 1960s and 1970s, for example.[42] These traditions assign high importance to project- and problem-based learning, interdisciplinary study, and a curriculum that has balance and breadth. A bolder, broader curriculum extending beyond the basics of literacy and numeracy has also characterized systems for decades in Scotland and many of the Nordic countries, as well as in some Canadian provinces, for example.

How do we keep on improving the details of our work while also transforming everything that we do? How do we get bolder in our educational ambitions while staying specific about how we achieve them and about how we do so without any sacrifice to foundational skills? And how do we embrace creativity, problem-solving, well-being and learning to live together sustainably, while also continuing to make progress for every young person in our care? These are some of the biggest both/and questions of our time that cannot be handled by mandates from the top, nor left to voluntary initiative by those on the front line. We need coherence without anarchy on the one hand or regimented alignment on the other. To achieve that, we need to get stuck into the middle.

Autonomy and Transparency

Educational reform has seen the rapid rise of two strategies to create higher standards of achievement in schools: *autonomy* and *transparency*. Both these strategies have honourable origins, but they have often been co-opted and corrupted to achieve purposes that are the very opposite of their original intentions. Let's begin with autonomy.

One of the worst states of human existence is no autonomy. Zero autonomy robs us of our ability to determine our own fate. Complete autonomy, in which anything and everything can be freely chosen, can be a kind of tyranny too.

When we have no autonomy, we have no freedom, choice, or responsibility. We are not autonomous. We are automatons. We are like robots, with no free will. Top-down standardization of curriculum, for example, takes away the capacities of teachers to create their own curriculum in ways that best meet the needs and circumstances of their students. It undermines the essence of professionalism: to exercise discretionary judgement in the interests of the people we serve.

In response to these problems, autonomy promises liberation from oppression – a shedding of the shackles. Autonomy offers choice, discretion, and self-determination. In the New Hampshire motto: it is "live free or die". But absolute or excess autonomy is in many ways as dangerous as no autonomy. In *The Paradox of Choice*, Barry Schwartz argues that complete or infinite choice is as much of a tyranny as no choice at all.[43] People become overwhelmed by the plethora of alternatives and endure anxiety as they must choose one option against endless others, including ones that might conceivably have been better. A restaurant menu that reads more like a book, a jeans shop with countless styles and cuts, and a selection of schools so wide that parents are terrified of making the wrong choice for their child – all these things characterize the tyranny of choice.

Unbridled freedom leads to incoherence in systems, inconsistency in provision, and inequality of educational opportunity as the privileged have more choices as well as greater capacity to act on them compared to the poor. This is also the criticism of unlimited professional autonomy for teachers: that teachers will be free to exercise poor judgement as well as good judgement, to teach according to their idiosyncratic passions rather than in line with the best evidence, to create gaps and duplications in children's education as these children move up the grades or their parents move around the country, and to be oblivious to each other's work rather than deliberately building upon it. Unregulated professional autonomy leads to inconsistency in innovation, imperviousness to scrutiny, and an educational world where enthusiasm doesn't always lead to excellence.

The answer to these excesses of free will and determinism in teaching has been to promote combinations of autonomy and control. One of these involves professional transparency. When something is transparent, you can see through it, like glass. Transparency consists of accuracy, clarity, and openness or visibility. In the social world, transparency emerged as a way of making political and corporate power holders more accountable. It was used by the public and its democratic institutions to hold elites in check. Corporate transparency ensures that the accounts of powerful companies are open not only to shareholders, but also to public scrutiny.[44] Environmental transparency deters companies from discharging toxic pollutants that imperil public health and safety.

In education, getting increased transparency seems an unassailable answer to top-down, punitive accountability. It promotes openness, inquiry, better communication, and shared responsibility for improvement. Or does it? In business and the environment, transparency originated as a strategy to hold the powerful to account. In education, though, it now often operates in the other direction. Data-driven transparency has been used as a tool to watch over the professional practice of teachers and to have teachers constantly watching over each other.[45]

Transparency is not a substitute for trust or even a precondition for it. In their research on school districts that make effective use of data for improvement, for example, University of California San Diego professors, Amanda Datnow and Vicki Park, found that effective and transparent uses of data occur in districts where there is already high trust and stable leadership.[46] Transparency builds on pre-existing relationships of high trust and leadership stability. It is not a substitute or even a springboard for these things. Trust is a prerequisite for effective transparency, not an outcome of it. Indeed, where there is already pervasive mistrust and unstable leadership, transparency only creates suspicion about the motives behind it (to remove unwanted teachers, perhaps) or about the unreliable nature of the indicators that underpin it (such as value-added measures of achievement). Many teachers see through these imposed efforts to increase transparency.

Downward transparency occurs when people in power look down at those beneath them to see their performance from above. Downward transparency is the executive suite's glass floor. More data in the form of published test scores or regular learning walks through teachers' classrooms create constant surveillance and top-down control.

By contrast, *lateral transparency* occurs when it is peers who see each other's practices and results.[47] Comparing publicized performance data from different schools, subjects, or grade levels, as well as employing procedures for teachers to observe and provide feedback on each other's classrooms, make teaching less of a mutual mystery.

Upward transparency occurs when holders of power in political or corporate life are required to disclose information to those beneath them about expenses, accounting, contracts, hiring decisions, environmental impact, and so forth. Upward transparency is designed to protect the public and prevent misuses of power. It is an effort to hold leaders accountable, so their glass floor becomes everyone else's see-through ceiling.

When upward and downward transparency are in balance, we have reciprocal accountability. But upward transparency, or what is called *sousveillance* (watching from below), is often lacking in the education profession.[48] While teachers may find they are perpetually evaluated according to continuous streams of performance data from above, the practices and effectiveness of school principals and superintendents are less open to examination from below. Too often, transparency is about being able to see more clearly what is beneath us or around us. It should also be about looking up to examine and expose the actions of those above. It's time to take the lid off transparency.

Transparency is not an end unto itself. Its purpose, in education, should be as a tool to secure improvement as well as some degree of accountability. Lateral transparency, as well as two-way vertical transparency, offer answers here, but only where there is also a strong commitment to building trust in an educational community. Transparency challenges individual autonomy by opening people's practice to scrutiny. But transparency is also open to misuse by the hierarchy. To avoid these problems, transparency seems to require the pre-existence of trust and shared responsibility for both participation in change and for the results of any changes. Building trust and developing responsibility are tasks that cannot be discharged from above, but ones that somehow need to be coordinated, orchestrated, and given coherence, among people, in and around the middle.

Conclusion

In this day and age, leadership is intensely paradoxical. Of course, paradox is a timeless quality of almost all leadership. How can you be humble without making yourself so small that you cannot advocate effectively for the people you serve? How can you be present and visible, yet also protect your own needs for solitude and renewal? How can you be inclusive without being indecisive?

Other paradoxes of leadership have a more contemporary feel to them. Crises like the Big Five omni-crisis of plague, war, climate change, racism, and the threat to democracy bring them upon us in multitudes. In climates of bitter division and rancour, how do you appease one group without offending another one? How do you promote creative innovation without harming test scores and examination results? What happens to your commitments to equity when some of the religious communities you serve hold beliefs that are homophobic or that treat women as having fewer rights than men?

One answer is to admit and accept that these things can't be done – not perfectly anyway. Leaders can't know everything about everyone and everything. Data and research don't always provide the solutions. Professional judgement calls are matters of human calculation, not mathematical precision. They are based on experience and intuition as much as facts and statistics. In a way, imperfect leadership is the essence of professionalism. If the imperfections are collective rather than individual, they increase the prospects of getting things right, and of taking collective responsibility rather than assigning personal blame when we don't.

Another way of dealing with dilemmas, conflicts and crises is to treat them in a non-binary way where options are not mutually exclusive. Both/and thinking, that John Dewey pioneered in education, requires empathy, ingenuity, and integrity. Empathy comes from the leader's quest to genuinely understand different and even opposing interests and viewpoints. Ingenuity is found in a group's capacity to devise original solutions that advocates of opposing positions have not previously considered, in search of common agreement and a shared direction. And integrity is about making sure that creative solutions are not immoral or illegal, but that they are consistent with core values. A strategic pivot is fine. Moral capitulation is not.

This chapter has examined three kinds of both/and thinking as they apply to educational change in a volatile world – integrating top-down reform with bottom-up innovation (though this is also a metaphor I will revisit and revise shortly), seeking wholesale transformations that do not sacrifice incremental gains, and using transparency to boost people's sense of shared autonomy instead of it becoming another way to exercise top-down surveillance.

The next chapter explores how to try and occupy some sort of middle ground that sits between and beyond competing extremes and disconnected levels of administration and management. It takes us into the middle.

3

LEADING IN THE MIDDLE

Looking to the Middle

One of the consequences of putting too much emphasis on control at the top, even when it is combined with freedom to innovate at the bottom, is that it has bypassed the middle. This has led to incoherence across entire systems. Engaging the middle is essential. Without it the top lacks first-hand knowledge of practice in the schools, and the bottom lacks colleagues who can communicate and connect people to what is happening in other schools.

Because of the limitations of top-down reform and bottom-up innovation in education, a few systems have started to create an intermediary or middle layer of processes and relationships that will pass along changes from the top, gather up innovations from the bottom, and even make and manage changes themselves.

Looking at what's going on in the middle and trying to improve it often doesn't get the respect it deserves, though. Doing something about the middle can feel more like a secondary concern or an afterthought. It only happens when everything else has been put in place.

The very way the idea of the middle is presented in everyday language is a symbol of the overall problem. Often, "the middle" seems less interesting than the end points of a continuum. Middle child. Middle school. Middle age. Middle-aged spread. Middle Earth. Middle Kingdom. Middle America. Middle England. Piggy in the middle. Monkey in the middle. Stuck in the middle. Middle class. Middle of the road. Fair to middling. The same phenomenon

DOI: 10.4324/9781315682921-3

also exists in languages and cultures other than English. Swedes, for instance, refer to middle milk (semi-skimmed) and middle beer (between strong and light).

The middle is also often regarded as a connector, like a middle school, that exists in between elementary and high, or primary and secondary. When people talk about a middle level or middle tier, it's a struggle to give the middle an identity of its own. Be honest. If you put in your dating app profile that you are in *middle management*, do you really think hordes of potential suitors will swipe right in response?

This chapter and the next analyse efforts to attend to the middle in locally elected school districts (elsewhere known variously as school boards, municipalities, local authorities, or prefectures). I outline the traditional promise and purposes of school districts in the middle of large systems. I also consider criticisms of their limitations and of whether they have outlived their purpose in the volatile and complex environment that exists today. Then I turn to wilful attempts to reduce or eliminate the role of school districts for political and financial purposes that have little to do with educational improvement or innovation. Finally, I look at the subsequent rise of new middle level structures and processes to link the top to the bottom of educational change efforts. The following chapter then sets out a more inclusive, empowering, and systemically effective approach called *Leadership From the Middle*.

The Traditional Role of the Middle

Historically, school districts have been a mechanism to get communities involved with and responsible for educating their children and adults. They have done this within broad parameters of policy and funding set out by central governments. Community members elect representatives, council members, or trustees to oversee policy and directions within the school and an elected or appointed executive takes a strong role in leading progress in those directions. Staffing, professional learning and development, promotion, innovation, advice and inspection, transportation, aspects of curriculum development, safeguarding of children, allocation of children to schools, and support for special educational needs are among the many functions that districts have performed in the interests of the children that the local community should, ideally, know best.

Districts can accomplish many important purposes. They can define a focus for school improvement and be a means for efficient and effective use of research evidence across schools. School districts provide support so schools can respond coherently to multiple external reform demands and they can be champions for families, students, and their communities, making sure everyone is treated fairly. Research on strong school districts has shown they can be powerful forces for positive educational change. Steadily improving districts like Boston in Massachusetts and Long Beach in California have received widespread acclaim for their system-wide gains.[1] In *Achieving Coherence in District Improvement*, Harvard University professor, Susan Moore Johnson, and her colleagues, found that districts that achieve the greatest coherence have stability of leadership, establish a clear vision, and secure collaborative involvement of educators.[2] In England, some urban districts, like the London boroughs of Hackney and Tower Hamlets, went from being the lowest performers in the country, to scoring above the national average on multiple indicators.[3]

In many countries, districts have been the backbone and the heart and soul of democratic school systems. At its best, local democracy is vibrant and immensely relevant to the people participating in it. Few things matter more in a community than the well-being of its families and the future of its children.

The Sagging Middle

Despite their long traditions and examples of notable accomplishment, school districts, like central governments and individual schools, are not always strong. Some districts do well while others fare badly. Districts vary in their resources and capacities for change like networking and seeking out other ideas. Districts can be self-serving, politically toxic, glacially slow at driving improvement, and, sometimes, just downright corrupt. Some districts are so tiny that they are almost literally incestuous.

In the United States and England especially, there have been unacceptable variations in quality among school districts. Due to differences in demographics, poverty levels, funding, and associated variations in capacity to develop effective leadership, very high performing and very low performing districts sometimes coexist side-by-side.[4] Redistricting – redrawing the boundaries of districts – sometimes deliberately exacerbates these problems by lumping the poorest or most racially minoritized part of the population together in one (underfunded) district such as an inner city, while more prosperous communities in suburban peripheries are clustered together in another designated district. The upshot is a conundrum: although all educationally high performing democracies are characterized by strong local control, not all nations with strong local control are high performing.

Over the last three decades, the position and legitimacy of school districts have come under threat. There are three reasons for this: whether people have available time to participate properly in the governance of districts, whether their levels of expertise are sufficient for the complex issues facing schools today, and whether culture wars and identity politics are dividing people in districts rather than uniting them.

Time

Many people do not have as much time for elected public service of a voluntary or low paid nature, as it often is, as was once the case. More and more women work outside the home. People also spend more hours working in their jobs and careers. Middle-class careers can be extremely demanding when people feel they must work harder and longer to keep up and try to stay ahead. Meanwhile, among the lower paid, two or three jobs are often required just to make ends meet. An expanding cohort of retired people does have more time for volunteering, but although grandparents can be highly valued sources of support for children and their families, they are often out of tune with the needs of modern families, or less knowledgeable about teaching and learning and the way schools work compared to their own schooldays.

Expertise

Like everything else, education has changed and continues to change. Teaching and learning are a far cry from the lone teacher standing in front of the class, setting individual tasks, and organizing occasional groupwork. Pedagogically, teaching is considerably more complex than it once was. Practice is more evidence-based, requiring people who make decisions about it to upskill themselves with technical knowledge and expertise. Special needs diagnoses and strategies are professionally sophisticated and require specialized medical, legal, and psychological knowledge to manage them. Children's well-being now depends on more than teachers who are caring and kind. It requires command of safeguarding procedures, familiarity with risk assessments, and awareness of specific strategies to improve well-being such as building resilience, emotional regulation, and dealing with trauma. Digitally based learning is also an increasing part of school life and hard enough even for qualified teachers to master, sometimes. For some sections of the lay population, how learning technologies can be used thoughtfully and effectively is even more challenging. In a world where education is becoming more and more politicized, policies change dramatically every time governments do, and keeping up with endless waves of policy mandates can consume immense amounts of time, even among qualified professionals. The result, according to Henry Smith, former assistant Secretary of Education in President Clinton's administration, is that "It often looks more like the school boards are managed by school administrators instead of the other way around."[5] Perhaps the job is now beyond the capacity of most people in local control of their schools.

Culture Wars

Educational decision-making has become more political and divisive. School communities are more diverse in race, language, religion, and culture. Schools also pay more attention to diversities that have always

been there, such as neurodiversity (including autism, attention defi-
cit disorders, and so on), gender-based identities, and the needs and
contributions of indigenous persons. Inclusion of different perspectives
and traditions can lead to heated arguments and bitter divisions about
what should be included in or excluded from an already overcrowded
curriculum, or about whether more competency-based curricula
threaten the traditional canons of subject knowledge that some parents value. Fake news, culture wars, conspiracy theories, and the online
spread of fear, anxiety, and hate – all of them horrible accompaniments
to the Big Five omni-crisis – can push school district members and
their communities into devoting disproportionate amounts of time to
fighting over very specific hot-button issues such as the installation of
gender-neutral bathrooms, the use of culturally controversial texts, the
treatment of colonization and slavery in the teaching of history, or the
retention or not of creationism in the science curriculum.[6] Alongside
these questions, and in the face of the professionally complex nature of
the education agenda, some school district members also understand-
ably home in on issues that don't seem to have changed and that they
more easily understand, such as school bus schedules, behaviour policies, sports competitions, and dress codes.

Especially in systems made up of many small, rural communities,
where there are numerically limited pools of talent for elected districts
to draw upon, there is a growing belief that locally elected districts can
no longer handle the scope and sophistication of educational decision-
making in the twenty-first century. The US state of New Jersey, with
a population close to nine million, has almost 600 school districts.[7]
The Czech Republic, with a population exceeding ten million, has
over 6,000 self-governing municipalities responsible for education –
an overreaction, perhaps, to the one-size-fits-all policies of the Soviet
era.[8] Tiny Iceland, which is made up of barely a third of a million
people, has 74 school municipalities – about the same number as
Ontario with a population that is almost 40 times greater.[9] In a globally advanced world perhaps these levels of local democracy may be
just too local to be effective.

When communities like these become fixated on single issues and
get distracted from the broader agenda of improving their schools
for every child, governments find it increasingly hard to get policies

implemented. No wonder, then, that some of them become impatient with local school districts, get frustrated about their very existence, and wish they could do without them altogether. One former Minister of Education I have worked with, who was passionate about achieving greater equity and inclusion, and who felt that districts were implementing government priorities far too slowly, once blurted out in ironic exasperation that if they had their way, they would put school districts up against a wall and shoot them!

The Canadian province of Nova Scotia has taken a less hyperbolic stance. But it has certainly been more decisive. It abolished all but one of its school districts entirely. This decision followed a 2018 system review of educational performance the province had commissioned from a former Ontario educational policy leader, Dr Avis Glaze.[10] Although Glaze wrote that she valued the contribution of service and dedication that school districts expressed at their best, she criticized the ineffectiveness of districts in Nova Scotia in terms of "dysfunction, turf wars, mistrust, lack of communication, inconsistency in terms of curriculum and outcomes, and ultimately a failure to move the school system forward".[11] The current system, Glaze continued, was "playing catch-up when it comes to goals of 21st century education" that was distracting it from focusing on student achievement and on "the capacity building to make this possible".[12] As a result, Glaze's recommendation, swiftly implemented by the government, was that "the seven . . . regional school boards should be eliminated" because of

> confused, unclear roles and responsibilities; a wide variety of performance from board to board; too many conflicting policies; transparency issues; an unhealthy level of acclaimed candidates and a lack of fresh voices; constituents not knowing their local board members, nor the roles they played, and so on.[13]

Hollowing Out the Middle

One response to these problems facing school districts is to say that districts are not worth saving. Instead, reforms should be delivered in detail from the top, or policies should be determined in a market-based system of individual schools or branded chains of schools like US charter schools, Swedish free schools, and English academies. These schools can operate free from district control and from teacher union regulations, which, ironically, also makes them more amenable to top-down control.

This alternative proposes that school districts must be considerably weakened or eliminated altogether because they interfere with a more market-based model of public education. The model rests on central governments advancing and imposing private or semi-private owner-ship of schools, on creating profit-making opportunities for private sector interests, and on competitive school choice that favours elite parents and their children over others with fewer economic or cultural resources.

This strategy has had a huge impact on the growth of free schools and academies in England and Sweden, and on the charter school movement in the United States. It has also led to a serious decline in intermediary local and democratic control of public education. Districts have been bypassed by reducing their funding, curtailing their responsibilities, or eliminating them altogether. Yet, in all three countries, the attack on school districts to stimulate privatization and competition, and to remove obstruction to central government policies, has led to no overall improvement in student learning and achievement.

In *Slaying Goliath: The Passionate Resistance to Privatization and the Fight to Save America's Public Schools*, former US assistant secretary of education, Diane Ravitch, documents extensive research which shows that, in general, charter schools do not raise achievement or narrow achievement gaps better than public schools.[14] A highly cited US Department of Education funded study reported that middle schools designated as charters that held parent lotteries for entrance were "neither more nor less successful than traditional public schools in improving student achievement".[15] Summarizing research in the area, the US National Conference of State Legislatures has concluded that charter schools are "not, on average, better or worse in student perfor-mance than the traditional public-school counterparts", nor, contrary to the hopes of their founders, have they innovated more rapidly than regular public schools.[16]

Two US economists have also completed some of the most definitive research of the impact on student achievement of the movement
from local authorities to individual academies organized as chains of
"multi-academy trusts" (MATs) in England. Helen Ladd and Edward
Fiske concluded that

> while some local authorities are decidedly weak, it is hard to make the case
> that the basic system of local authorities is failing.[17] Moreover, some local
> authorities, including many in London, have done an outstanding job of
> assuring high-quality schools for most of their primary school students.

Likewise, research by the UK's Sutton Trust finds no clear evidence
that chains of academies outperform traditional locally controlled
schools.[18] Ladd and Fiske note that MATs and similar chain-like
structures of cross-school organization in England "seriously undermine the[se] mechanisms for responsiveness to local concerns". The
new system

> effectively strips local authorities of responsibility for many of the func-
> tions related to articulating overall community needs, coordinated
> planning, assuring high quality schools for all children in the area, and
> accountability to parents. The new system is ill equipped to replace
> authorities as providers of these functions.[19]

Denuding and diminishing local authorities or local school districts therefore leads to no proven gains in achievement or equity
overall. It only contributes to deterioration in local support, the quality of services, and accountability to the community. Moreover, this
movement towards having schools in chains and trusts that afford
parents greater choice, at the expense of local community engagement and control, does not even lead to parents becoming more satisfied with their children's schools. In England, families can name
up to six state schools for their children to attend. In Scotland, by
contrast, most children still go to their local state schools in one
of the country's 32 local authorities or districts. A study by Aveek
Bhattacharya, published in the *Journal of Social Policy* in 2022, found
that it was the Scottish families who were more likely to be satisfied

with their choice of school. "This research adds to the growing evidence that school choice policies have failed to bring the benefits they were supposed to", he wrote. "Parents offered a range of options for their children's school are no happier than parents who have less choice about education."[20]

A global pioneer of the move towards privatization and the downgrading of the size and influence of school districts is Sweden. In 1992, Sweden introduced vouchers to enable parents to send their children to regular local district schools, or private, mainly for-profit "free" schools. The largest owners of these free schools today are hedge fund companies who quickly realized that the return on investment in free schools was greater and more stable (due to government backing and protection) than the return on investments in financial markets. About one-fifth of Swedish students now go to free schools.[21]

What have been the consequences? By the time the free school system had become embedded, the OECD's PISA tests of 15-year-old students recorded the fastest decline between 2002 and 2012 of any developed economy, registering Sweden as the lowest performer with greater inequities than any of the neighbouring Nordic countries.[22] Sweden's wild west approach to educational change led to great inconsistencies of quality and provision and, in 2015, an OECD report of Sweden's performance and progress pointed to "weak and unclear" accountability of the system.[23] Defenders of the free school system have pointed to other possible explanations for declining performance such as progressive teaching methodologies, and low pay and status for teachers.[24] But even if these other explanations are also valid, the shift to a market system, and the weakening of traditional school districts, often by leaving them with disproportionate responsibility for low-income and immigrant student populations, has improved neither equity nor quality in the system.

In all three cases – the United States, England, and Sweden – hollowing out the middle through market-driven reforms has not worked. Quality has not improved, inequities have not decreased, and the teaching profession has become increasingly demoralized, leading to major problems of recruitment and retention in all three countries. One response has been to try and improve accountability and coherence in the system by inserting a new system of responsibility and control "in the middle" to replace the influence once exerted by democratically elected local school districts.

Leading *In* the Middle

Where there is strong direction from government, along with market competition among schools, creating a new middle level of organization to replace that of local school districts provides a possible way to plug the policy implementation gap between a central government and hosts of individual or loosely organized schools. The idea of introducing a middle level or middle tier in school systems has therefore become increasingly attractive, not just within the three countries just discussed, but also, as this new policy narrative has gained traction, in other countries and systems too.

In a report for the Massachusetts Business Alliance in Education about the future of education, Sir Michael Barber and his colleagues argued for a new middle tier to replace the traditional middle stratum of democratically elected school districts. This report referred to earlier work with Barber's colleagues at McKinsey & Company where they identified "a critical role" for what they called the "middle tier". This had four components:

- To "provide targeted support to schools and monitor compliance".
- To "facilitate communication between schools and the center".
- To "encourage inter-school collaboration".
- To "*moderate community resistance to change* by making the case for a different future" (my emphasis).[25]

This idea of a *middle tier* is part of an explicit effort to minimize local democratic control and the public's possible opposition to central government policies. This middle serves as a conduit to pass on policies and to get compliance. It also acts as a buffer to insulate policy makers from parents or community activists who might otherwise question or challenge their leadership.

Other cases for middle level or middle tier leadership have emphasized the importance of coherence in school systems. For example,

Michael Fullan has described what he also calls *Leading From the Middle* (even though it is really *In* the Middle) as:

> a deliberate strategy that increases the *capacity* and internal *coherence* of the middle as it becomes a more effective *partner upward* to the state and *downward* to its schools and communities, in pursuit of greater *system performance*. . . . This approach is powerful because it mobilizes the middle (districts and/or networks of schools), thus developing widespread capacity [my emphases].[26]

Andreas Schleicher, Director for Education and Skills for the OECD, has also argued for a stronger role for the "meso" or middle level of change in school systems.[27] For him, the middle helps to implement changes from the top, and moves around ideas and strategies that are percolating up from beneath. The middle improves efficiency, performance, and coherence by breaking down the walls of miscommunication and misunderstanding that can otherwise pervade large organizations like school systems.

In all these cases, middle level or middle tier leadership is a role or function that creates coherence, increases efficiency, and enhances performance in a complex system. This idea especially applies where democratically controlled districts have been weakened to remove restrictions to market competition and centralized control. Leading *In* the Middle in such settings is about creating more efficient and, sometimes, more competitive systems, not building better democratic and professional communities. What does this new kind of middle look like in practice?

- Owner-managed *networks, chains, or trusts* bind schools together, usually across geographic regions, with the corporate vision and identity of one brand, under an overall manager or director.
- *Regional departments* of central government do the coordinating work that districts used to do but with closer alignment between local and central strategy, and therefore a greater likelihood of success in implementing central government policies. Examples are Nova Scotia and states in Australia.
- *Professional networks* move ideas around the overall system, or they create energy and motivation among committed teachers

to implement new initiatives in curriculum, pedagogy, or digital learning technologies, for example. Governments initiate or support these new structures.

Each of these middle level entities has drawbacks, though. A *chain, trust, or brand* brings about a kind of corporate loyalty to an idea or way of working and even to the mutual success of all schools that are part of the brand. But it doesn't usually strengthen local communities. Brands compete rather than collaborate with each other. They also compete with schools that remain under traditional district control. The community's capacity becomes weakened and divided. The historic role of schools as beating hearts of their communities is undercut. Brands and chains supplant places and communities. Borderless worlds of educational provision are created that suit privileged families but weaken the community bonds that are important for everyone else.

Replacing one or more districts with a *regional department of government* enables on-the-ground management to connect with local communities and schools more coherently but only when they are aligned with government policy. What happens now, in a democracy, where community members are dissatisfied with their government's actions? What if indigenous or immigrant communities are not properly consulted or catered for? What if allocations of special needs support are insensitive or insufficient? Community members now have no one to turn to among their elected representatives to be their champions and take on the government if they need to. All that is available is a regional arm of government that may be the very source of the problem it is supposed to resolve. University of Ottawa colleague, Jess Whitley, and I heard these kinds of concerns in Nova Scotia after districts were replaced by regional administration.[28]

Last, while, as we will see, teacher and school networks can be powerful drivers of positive change, this potential can be quickly compromised when the *networks* are initiated and *managed by government departments* that regard the networks as tools for implementing government policy, not as incubators of school-driven innovation. Government-controlled networks lack the sophistication of mature networks that become, in many ways, self-organizing and self-improving. Instead, networks turn into clusters of schools organized around hubs of government leadership. They find themselves constantly having to return to that hub, whenever they want to initiate new activity. Most teachers eventually mistrust these bureaucratic hub-and-spoke networks. Some years ago, educators I worked with in Australia cynically renamed their cluster leaders as duster cleaners! These bureaucratically appointed cluster leaders ultimately come to be regarded and resisted as just one more tool of top-down control.

In 2018, Drs Toby Greany and Rob Higham from University College London's Institute of Education reported on a detailed study of interactions, networks and collaborations among 47 schools and how they operated as a "middle tier" of improvement and change in the English education system. In England's complicated system, they discovered, middle tier forms of organization often overlapped and intersected. Schools could be part of a MAT, involved in several networks, and under regional government administration all at the same time. Individually and in combination, they learned, all these forms of middle tier organization "diminished local knowledge about schools" and lacked a "clear, democratic mandate".[29] Many parts of the middle tier had become highly commercialized, they found. When government funding was tight, many schools developed "trading arms" to provide professional development or assist other schools. This, in turn, tended to make the middle tier focus on short-term improvement strategies that would lift results quickly, or on providing knowledge and expertise that could be "easily codified and commodified" as products and packages rather than supporting deeper learning among students, teachers, and leaders.[30]

Locally, schools developed "status hierarchies" in terms of their esteem and popularity among parents. This inhibited their ability to work together for the common good of the community. Nationally, as talent and initiative surfaced in different parts of the middle tier, some leaders took on national leadership responsibilities, only to find they were now part of a "co-opted elite of nationally designated school system leaders".[31]

Greany's and Higham's conclusion is that "there are now multiple sub-systems, with different, partially overlapping 'middle tier' organizations that hold diverse views on how the school system should be organized".[32] In other words, efforts to create new structures of leading in the middle in a partially privatized system have led neither to improved achievement, nor to greater coherence.

The key elements that describe the aspirations of *Leading In the Middle* are summarized in Table 3.1.

Table 3.1 Leading In the Middle

Leading In the Middle
Level, layer or tier
Improving performance
Better systems
Coherence and connection
Implementing initiatives

The aspirations of *Leading In the Middle* seem to have fallen far short of the actual outcomes on the ground, though. In market systems, or systems focused on narrowly defined government priorities such as literacy and mathematics, *Leading In the Middle*, through chains and trusts, networks or clusters, or units of regional administration, has often been about improving measured student achievement. It has also been about ensuring fidelity with top-down government priorities.

Initially conceived as a method to improve the efficiency of market-driven systems under central government control where local democracy has been weakened or eliminated, the principles of *Leading In the Middle* have spread to other countries and systems that are also seeking greater coherence. But, as we shall see in the next chapter, in a democracy, *Leading In the Middle* is not the only or best method of bringing about positive change, improvement, or local participation. A better strategy is *Leadership From the Middle*.

The End of the Middle?

Is it all up for *Leading In the Middle*, then? Are districts doomed because their local communities of overworked and unavailable people don't have the time or expertise to participate effectively in a fast-paced, highly complex, and increasingly contentious world? And are market-driven chains, brands, and networks unable to mesh with top-down government policies that are always changing, often contradictory, and too inflexible to respond to a never ending omni-crisis? Can we no longer trust our people? Are their capacities being outmatched by a world that is mainly beyond their comprehension? Do we need to turn to strong leaders to guide us through the chaos, and defer to their policies and demands? Or should we let science, data, and artificial intelligence guide us instead? Is *Leading In the Middle*, either through districts, or through networks and chains, a good idea whose time has passed?

The next chapter takes a less despairing path by arguing that people's capacities can be developed. Collectively, it argues, with the right direction and strategy, we can become stronger together. We can Lead *From* the Middle not just to connect and coordinate agendas set by leaders at the top, but to empower people to develop their own changes and improvements that are responsive to their local communities in a turbulent and unpredictable world.

4

LEADING DISTRICTS FROM THE MIDDLE

The Middle as the Core

The middle is a less important or inferior place to be in many languages and cultures. But this is not true in all of them. In Arabic cultures, for example, the middle is the best place of all. In Buddhism, it's the perfect point of balance and harmony. The Greek philosopher, Aristotle, encouraged us to seek out the "golden mean" in all things.[1]

If we reposition the middle to think of it not as an intermediary point between other things, but as the centre or core of something, as in a circle, it takes on very different connotations. The middle here may be the centre, the core, the beating heart, the soul, and the guts of leadership; the place where we find its substance and constitution. It's time to reconsider and reposition the middle; to give it pride of place rather than lowly status as a connector of other things or a compromise between them.

The Origin of Leadership From the Middle

Although the concept of *Leading From the Middle* or *Leadership From the Middle* is somewhat new, it is not distinctly mine. I first came across it in 2009 after I had been approached by the Ontario Council of Directors of Education (CODE) – equivalent to US school district superintendents – to work collaboratively with a consortium of ten school districts. They wanted a retrospective investigation into their efforts to improve school inclusion among students with special needs.

50

DOI: 10.4324/9781315682921-4

The districts felt they had been successful, but they had difficulty explaining why, even to them themselves. Over four years, my co-investigator, Henry Braun, and I, along with a graduate student team, helped the consortium understand and articulate how their strategy had enabled them to narrow achievement gaps for several minoritized and previously underserved populations.[2]

It was leaders of the consortium who named their strategy *Leading From the Middle*. They used this term to describe situations where districts developed their own strategies to promote inclusion of all students in ways that suited the diversities of their own communities. Using a unique design, that I will describe shortly, districts then networked and circulated these strategies among themselves. This circulation of knowledge occurred in an environment of transparent collective responsibility for participation and results. A core principle underpinning the approach was that *what is essential for some students is good for all students*. Assistive technologies and student self-advocacy, for example, are good not just for those with identified learning disabilities, but for all students who want to enhance their learning with technology, or to have more of a voice in articulating how they learn best. This principle was known as *Essential for Some, Good for All* (ESGA).

From 2014 to 2018, I was invited to resume collaboration with the consortium – this time with my colleague Dennis Shirley and another graduate student team – to determine what had happened and could continue to happen to *Leading From the Middle*.[3] The consortium decided to focus on selected district-by-district projects related to new government priorities concerned with broad excellence, equity, and well-being. Details of both projects, involving case studies, interviews, surveys, and documentary sources, are described in peer-reviewed articles elsewhere.[4]

Leadership From the Middle as Cross-District Collaboration

During the period addressed by our first project, the Ontario government, as we have seen, had concentrated on raising achievement and narrowing achievement gaps in measured performance in literacy and mathematics. There was a lot of top-down imposition of tests and a rather structured literacy programme, but the reform was also

accompanied by intensive coaching support and professional development for all elementary school teachers – particularly for teachers and
schools that struggled to hit the targets for proficiency.

The strategy met with considerable success – leading to gradual and
sustainable rather than suspiciously sudden improvements in measured
performance over several years. But the reform would have stood little
chance of success unless it could also motivate education professionals. Moreover, not everything that was required in the reform could be
encompassed by tests, targets, programmes, training, and coaching.

In terms of professional motivation, the government in the early
2000s had been dealt a dream hand by its political predecessors who
had presided over an era of austerity, chaotic curriculum reforms, a
climate of disrespect for teachers and the teaching profession, and a
resulting series of disputes with the teacher unions. If you want to
get a good reception for your policy, it's best to follow a bad one.
Austerity was replaced by investment. Collaboration replaced conflict. Educators started to feel valued rather than disparaged. But the
Liberal government that was elected in 2002 went further than simply
putting a stop to the bad things. It also allocated about C$25 million
to each of the teacher unions and the principal associations to stimulate motivation and commitment.[5]

The teacher unions used these resources to partner with the
Ministry of Education and build a national network of collaborative
teacher teams that undertook innovations in teaching and learning
that were then shared among them.[6] This injected energy into the
system and, as our own work with Ontario districts unfolded, some
of the most innovative projects we would see that were designed to
promote inclusion and well-being, had begun with this teacher innovation network. The principals, meanwhile, focused on leadership
initiatives to support student success through projects and conferences at which senior ministry staff, ministers, and sometimes the
province's premier were highly visible.[7]

Initially, though, the provincial government overlooked the school
districts and their leaders as a parallel opportunity for investment and
innovation. After representation from district leaders, the government
eventually allocated C$25 million to the districts too – to support
developing the government's inclusion strategy with the goal of reducing achievement gaps for students with identified special needs.[8]

With a population exceeding 14 million, and almost 5,000 schools, Ontario has 72 school boards (districts). These disaggregate into 31 English public boards, 4 French public boards, 29 English Catholic boards, and 8 French Catholic Boards.[9] School boards vary in size from tiny rural districts of three or four schools, to whole conurbations like the city of Toronto. They are controlled by elected trustees who appoint a director who largely leads and manages the professional agenda of the district. Unlike much of the United States, districts do not raise money through local taxes but are allocated provincial resources according to financial formulae based on size and need. There are still some inequities between types of districts in the same geographic area arising from covert forms of student selection. These include some Catholic districts accepting fewer students with severe special educational needs compared to their public counterparts, and the tendency for French immersion programmes to attract disproportionate numbers of families from higher socioeconomic backgrounds, for example. There are also some differences in teachers' and administrators' salaries between types of districts which are bargained separately, and in the relative ability of parents in affluent and less affluent districts to raise additional funds for school equipment and activities. However, the scale of these funding inequities is still smaller than in the more overtly unequal and competitive systems that operate in England, the United States, and Australia.

Just under 7 per cent of students in Ontario are enrolled in private schools – slightly less than the national average.[10] Like most provinces in Canada, there are also no equivalents of US charter schools, English academies, or Swedish free schools. For most Ontario families, the school their children attend is their local school that operates under district control, within the general parameters of a curriculum and assessment framework that is created and administered by the provincial administration. The provincial government has no direct authority over school districts and only intervenes in rare cases of financial mismanagement or collapses of governance.

In 2012, Dennis Shirley and I first introduced the concept of *Leading From the Middle* by describing the origins of this strategy in Ontario.[11] A summary of that argument, and of the supporting data, follows now. The Ontario government asked CODE's school district directors to lead professional development in order to implement a broad framework for inclusion, outlined in a 2005 policy document, *Education for All.*[12] This advanced increasingly accepted principles of inclusive education such as universal design for learning, differentiated instruction, and support for classroom teachers working in diverse learning environments. How would CODE implement a document that was philosophically inspiring but strategically also rather vague? A four-pronged strategy was adopted.

 Beginning in 2005, CODE distributed the government's resources equally across all districts, large and small, to build commitment among a critical mass of school district leaders, since three-quarters of Ontario's school districts are small or medium in size. "The funding was going to be equal, no matter the size of the district", the project's coordinator explained.

 Each district designed and developed its own inclusive education strategy to respond to the unique diversities of its own community – be this indigenous, Franco-Ontarian, immigrant, refugee, Old Order Mennonite, poor working class, and so on.

 A small team of retired superintendents and directors was appointed as a third-party organization to connect the districts with each other, circulate knowledge among them, and cultivate a sense of shared responsibility across them for all students' success. In the words of one member of this steering team, the strategy was about "bringing forth and empowering the knowledge that already existed with the superintendents".

 Districts were required to share the results of their efforts in face-to-face annual meetings.

In our 2009 interviews, one member of the coordinating team described these interrelated elements of the CODE strategy as "leading from the middle". Like many ideas in the work of my colleagues and myself, *Leading From the Middle* did not come from an experimental laboratory, or from theories originating in another field like business. It came from educators themselves. Essentially, *Leading From the Middle* encompassed seven principles that informed the districts' separate and combined change projects, as summarized in Figure 4.1.

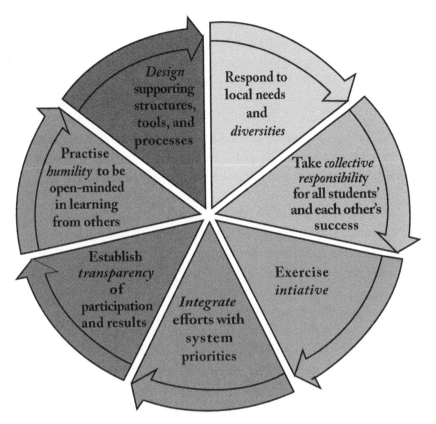

Figure 4.1 Seven Principles of Leading From the Middle[13]

Working with district directors and superintendents, we described the principles as follows:

1 *Responsiveness to diversity.*
  Districts and their schools generate solutions that respond to distinctive local needs and diversities through practices like differentiated instruction and Universal Design for Learning. *Leadership From the Middle* projects engage with students' distinctive identities and develop cooperation in schools to provide better support for students among special education support teachers, curriculum consultants, and regular classroom teachers.

2 *Responsibility.*
  Districts take collective responsibility for all students' success by working in professional learning communities. They examine student

data and bring together teachers with special education consultants, speech pathologists, and mental health specialists, to devise strategies to support all students who struggle with their learning. A culture of "my students" becomes a culture of "our students".

3 *Initiative.*
Leadership From the Middle is about implementing fewer initiatives and taking more initiative. Educators seize the initiative together to acknowledge and respond to challenges in their own schools and communities and to develop strategies to address them.

4 *Integration.*
Districts integrate their efforts with government priorities wherever possible, by linking to literacy reforms or efforts to close the achievement gap, for example.

5 *Transparency.*
Districts establish shared transparency of participation and results regarding their progress in improving learning, establishing well-being, and building identity. They share strategies and results with each other through their networks, relationships, and at public sessions that display their projects and their impact.

6 *Humility.*
No district sees itself as superior to the others. Each district demonstrates curiosity to learn from the rest. All districts commit to learning from other systems elsewhere.

7 *Design.*
Districts work together to ensure that principles are put in place through deliberate designs, and then disseminated throughout their schools and systems.

Leadership From the Middle doesn't give up on people's capacity to change, even when the circumstances are complex. Collaboration is the key. Teachers in schools and schools in a district work better when they collaborate. The principle of collaboration applies to districts too. Sharing strategies, seeking help, and moving ideas around helps everyone to improve over time.

Collaboration in ESGA didn't evolve by itself, though. It had a specific and deliberate architecture. The third-party steering committee of former superintendents connected districts with each other and moved ideas around them. Its members provided coaching and support in areas identified as needing improvement. Salaries were given to the coordinating committee and resources bought time and travel opportunity for leaders in the different districts and their schools. A culture of mutual help and support in an environment of humility where everyone recognized they had something to learn from their peers was modelled by the leadership and enhanced in common sessions of professional learning and transparency that brought all the districts together.

Small and somewhat isolated districts that may seem to have limited capacity learned and improved by connecting with each other and with larger districts that might otherwise have been disinclined to collaborate with districts much smaller than their own. Instead of eliminating districts because they struggle with small size and isolated geography, *Leadership From the Middle* invested in their professional capital and especially their social capital of collaboration by allocating extra funding and making them an integral and valued part of a wider community.[14] In other words, instead of regarding districts as obstacles to government attempts to implement policy, *Leadership From the Middle* strategies supported districts to generate changes that suited them and to spread these changes out for the benefit of others. The obstacle was no longer an obstacle. As Emperor Aurelius said, "What stands in the way becomes the way."[15]

Leadership From the Middle is much more than a tool to pass down policies from central government to the schools. It allows, encourages, and expects schools and districts to develop strategies of their own and then circulate them among other districts. For instance, when members of a French language district said that identity was as important as achievement in their minoritized culture, this became an important consideration for other schools and districts too. A climbing wall in a regular classroom was a place for students with foetal alcohol syndrome to go when they could not sit still any longer, but it was also useful for any student who needed to let off steam for a few minutes. What is essential for some can be good for all. This applies not only to different kinds of students, but also to different kinds of districts.

Finally, let's be clear. *Leadership From the Middle* works. We will see examples from other systems later. In Ontario alone, by working this way, between 2004–5 and 2010–11, reading scores improved by 13 per cent in public school districts, 11 per cent in Catholic districts and 21 per cent in Francophone districts. Writing scores improved by 20 per cent overall. Achievement gaps between students with identified special needs and other students narrowed by 8 per cent or more in reading, depending on the type of district, and 15 per cent or more for writing.[16]

Leadership From the Middle in Action

As our research developed in collaboration with the districts, it became clear that, compared to the period when ESGA was first being implemented, there was less orchestrated effort or investment on the part of the Ontario Ministry of Education to support a coordinated and continuing strategy of *Leadership From the Middle* across the districts. Resource allocations for leadership across and among the districts to continue work on inclusion were terminated. The key administrator (the Assistant Deputy Minister) in the province who had become the system's champion for *Leadership From the Middle* was recruited to be Director of one of Canada's largest school districts. *Leadership From the Middle* suffered the fate of many other promising innovations. After flourishing as a project supported with additional resources, it was eventually left without leadership or money.

In our project report and in our feedback to senior ministry leaders, we warned that without continued funding, *Leadership From the Middle* and all that it had promised would wither away. It would not sustain itself. If *Leadership From the Middle* was to be sustained across the whole system, we argued, budgets would need to be shifted from central government to structures and activities for inter-district collaboration. *Leadership From the Middle* would need to be an embedded and properly funded element of policy, not a transient project, a budgetary add-on, or a voluntary choice. Of course, suggestions to a central bureaucracy that it should slim itself down to empower those it serves are not among the most popular recommendations a research study can make!

Leadership From the Middle is not and cannot be self-sustaining. It must be nurtured and supported continuously by those at the top. It requires a structure of support, resources, and direction, as well as an embedded culture of shared habits and beliefs. With more than C$25 million of allocated government funding, ESGA galvanized all districts and their leaders to develop an inclusive strategy for students with special educational needs, that supported other students too, and that yielded clear gains in equity. Despite all this, the original collaboration among the 70-plus districts has largely faded away.

But this was not the end of *Leadership From the Middle*'s impact. Although it was no longer centre stage as a strategy of province-wide coherence and cohesion, it remained very much alive within the participating districts who continued working with us during the second phase of our collaborative work from 2014 to 2018. In effect, with our support, the ten consortium districts continued *Leadership From the Middle* among themselves.

At its consortium meetings, these ten districts worked with our research team to use the seven principles of *Leadership From the Middle* to organize the next phase of shared investigation and project development. Two examples in Figures 4.2 and 4.3 come from professional development work carried out with and by district leaders in a CODE Consortium meeting in 2015.

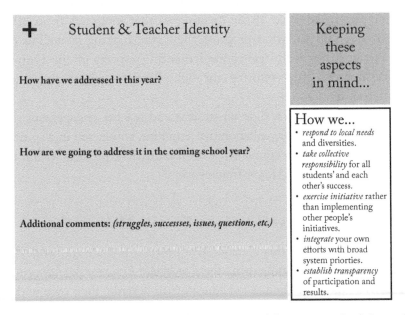

Figure 4.2 PowerPoint Slide Enabling Transparency of Activities on the Subject of Identity across the Consortium

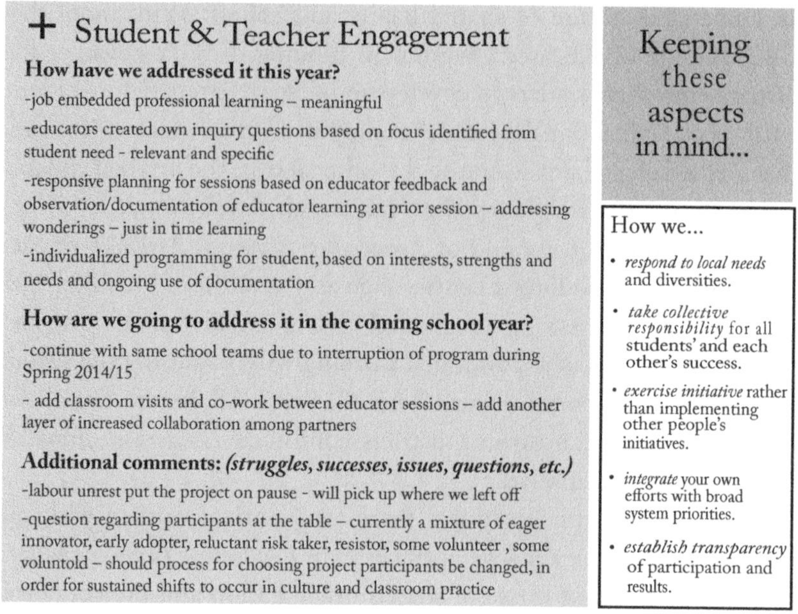

Figure 4.3 Sample Slide Exhibiting Transparency of One District's Activities on Student and Teacher Engagement

Consortium participants filled in the slides informed by the seven principles in advance of the meeting so that members from other districts could see what progress they were making as well as the challenges they were facing implementing aspects of the Ontario government's 2014 reforms through district projects they were undertaking.

Figure 4.3 shows a slide on student and teacher engagement that exemplifies how these collaborative activities, conducted in a spirit of shared inquiry, then connected with the districts' projects within the *Leadership From the Middle* framework.

The Three Meanings of Leadership From the Middle in Schools

Following on from this collaborative process to share the work that districts were developing using the *Leadership From the Middle* principles as a guide, we then asked educators to describe their own understandings of *Leadership From the Middle* as they experienced and had been experiencing it in their districts. It was time for them to reflect on the meaning that *Leadership From the Middle* had assumed in their own practice.

According to a Superintendent of Curriculum in one of the districts, *Leadership From the Middle* "kind of morphed into different things" over time. By 2014–18, even though *Leadership From the Middle* had less funding and no governmental support aside from encouragement and attendance of senior ministry staff at consortium meetings, it had assumed greater depth and complexity in relation to students, teaching and learning within the schools and districts themselves. It had become an embedded set of practices that varied in their structures and design yet were recognizable across all ten of the districts.

Successful and sustainable changes in organizations and even in entire societies require three things:

1 *A philosophy* that motivates people with a compelling purpose that gives them direction and moves them forward.
2 *A structure* of time, space, roles, and responsibilities that creates a framework to guide new action.
3 *A culture* of norms, beliefs, and habits that orders and orchestrates people's behaviour together.

These three components – philosophical, structural, and cultural – are evident in all kinds of changes, including *Leadership From the Middle*. To grasp their interrelated importance, let's consider an example outside education: the Dutch culture of cycling.

Look down from any office block in the Netherlands and you'll witness a vast sea of bicycles – some of them on the move, many parked in huge racks, hundreds at a time. The Dutch own more bicycles per capita than any other country in the world – almost twice the level of runner-up, Denmark. Children, adults, families, workers, students, people of all kinds are riding the streets in great numbers, miraculously not crashing into each other.[17]

Yet practically none of them are wearing helmets. In America and Canada, this is almost unthinkable. Not requiring your child to wear a helmet is a dereliction of parental duty. Often, it is illegal.

How is it that hospital Emergency Rooms in the Netherlands are not constantly filled with people who have broken their limbs or smashed their skulls – the result of riding recklessly without protection? It's got a lot to do with the place of cycling within the society. In the Netherlands, cycling is an everyday activity. It is gentle and inclusive, something that anyone and everyone can do. Cycling is steady. Riders are outdoors, enjoying the weather, looking around and taking in the scenery, keeping fit and healthy, possibly chatting to a cyclist beside them, and doing all this as part of everyday life. There are no special clothes for cycling – you just ride to and from school or the office in your skirt or your suit you'll be wearing that day. In the Netherlands, they say, you do not dress for the journey. You dress for the destination. It's like walking or gentle jogging on wheels. There are cycle lanes and stop lights everywhere. Cyclists, motorists, and pedestrians all obey them, each looking out for the other in the shared space they occupy together. It's one of the reasons why the Netherlands is top of the world on many global indicators of happiness and well-being.

In the United States and Canada, cycling to and from work is something fewer people do. It's treated more like an extreme sport. Except at the weekends, perhaps, cyclists put their work clothes in a backpack and gear up for their biking experience in tight cycling shorts, streamlining their bodies, getting up a head of speed, and building up a sweat. Non-cyclists in North America derisively refer to male cyclists of this ilk as MAMLS – Middle Aged Men in Lycra. They race to and from work, weaving in and out of traffic, cheating at the lights whenever they can, sneaking through on red, or going across sideways or even up the pavement so they don't have to stop. Motorists wave their fists at them in ire, and cyclists shout back when car drivers pull across their path or open a door without looking.

The whole thing is aggressive, competitive, and consumed with the North American obsession with speed and power. Each road user tries to steal the others' space. No one really trusts anybody else to be considerate, careful, or safe. In these societies, parents are right not to trust their children or anyone else to stay safe without the protection of a helmet. If you live in a society obsessed with speed and power, you'd be a fool to put your child or even yourself on a bike without proper protection.

What explains the positive and pervasive role of cycling in Dutch society? It hasn't evolved spontaneously. It is the result of a deliberate philosophy, structure and culture in the Netherlands that supports and sustains cycling as an everyday activity for everyone. Geography helps, of course. The Netherlands is a very flat country. Much of it was reclaimed from the sea. The country's highest point, far out on its south-eastern border, is barely more than 1,000 feet. The weather helps, too, with an equable climate, even in winter, that is moderated by the nearby presence of the North Sea. There are almost no mountains to climb in Dutch cycling, and, in the main, it is a year-round activity. But places with similar weather and geography, like eastern England, do not embrace the bicycle in the same way. Something else is also at play.

The Dutch have had a historic relationship with the bicycle, going back a hundred years. But by the 1960s, the growth of car ownership led to roads being built or redesigned for motorized traffic. Cycle use declined by over 10 per cent every two years. Accident rates increased, and in 1971, 400 children were killed in traffic accidents. An influential movement grew called *Stop de Kindermoord* (Stop the child murder!).

In the 1980s, Dutch cities responded by constructing vast networks of cycle paths. There are over 20,000 miles of them today. A quarter of all journeys are made by bicycle —nearly double that figure in the largest cities. When bicycling reaches a critical mass, everyone pays attention to it. Cyclists, motorists, and pedestrians all become aware of and considerate towards each other.

The transformation in the place of the bicycle in Dutch society and its huge contribution to the well-being of the nation's adults and children was built on a *philosophy* of historic bicycle use and the valuing of family well-being, on investment in a *structure* of networked cycleways and stop lights, and on a resulting *culture* of mutual trust and consideration for other users of roads and pathways.[18]

Every successful and sustainable organizational transformation requires attention to its *philosophy* of purpose, its *structure* that frames human interactions, and its *culture* that binds them together. It's the same, we found, for *Leadership From the Middle.*

A Philosophy of the Heart of Practice

Consortium educators viewed *Leadership From the Middle* as *their* concept, something that they had created and sustained even in the absence of government support. It was *their* initiative, not an initiative that came out of the ministry. They had developed it in a genuine spirit of collegiality, despite a year of labour unrest and other distractions. One director explained:

> To me, the essence of *Leading From the Middle* is making real your vision. It's about moving those ideas into concrete practice and making a positive difference, for all your students and for all your staff so that everybody just loves their learning environment. I don't see it as connected to personnel. I see that the whole notion of *Leading From the Middle* is a concept or a philosophy of wanting to get as close to the action as you possibly can.

In this view, *Leadership From the Middle* is not a location such as a middle tier. It means getting close to the teaching and learning that is at the heart of the profession. In the words of a mental health consultant, "Sometimes the middle is the students, sometimes the middle's the teacher. It depends on where learning is happening, or where the learning is." A Catholic district superintendent explained: "*Leading From the Middle* really speaks to us through our Catholic social teachings and that notion of subsidiarity – that the work and the change and the impact of that change will happen at the ground root."

Educators stated that *Leadership From the Middle* is about supporting students with all their diverse identities. "*Leading From the Middle* really forces us to look beyond those categories, those roles, to see how we can serve others to really uplift them." *Leadership From the Middle* as a vision or philosophy of practice that stayed close to students was evident when consortium educators identified "students of wonder" and studied their assets as well as their challenges. It was also manifest when students learned about the lives of missing indigenous women, studied inequities in water quality across communities, or brought a refugee family to their community after studying the refugee crisis in their social studies classes, for example.

Leadership From the Middle projects took shape in classrooms and schools when teachers strove to develop students' skills of self-advocacy in writing their own Individual Education Plans, when students were engaged in inquiring into and representing their own mental health issues, and when teachers assessed student's work by sitting beside them in processes of pedagogical documentation (a kind of assessment for learning) rather than using standardized tests to make data-driven interventions. These cheek-by-jowl forms of engaging students in reflecting on their own learning were also evident when forums were organized for all students to share their ideas about what could be done to improve school climate and when apps were designed that enabled students to inform educators when students were concerned about other students' lack of well-being. *Leadership From the Middle* was about placing students, their learning, and their well-being at the heart of and close to teachers' practice. This student-centered view of *Leadership From the Middle* provoked deeper reflection among educators about their beliefs, relationships, and strategies:

> What are our values? What are our customs? What are our beliefs? We know that it starts with the beliefs, and it results in a chain of events, a chain of thoughts, relationships that develop, connections that are made and actions that are planned and actions that are implemented. That becomes the work that we do collectively and that becomes the best that we achieve.

One district's administrative team represented their understanding of *Leadership From the Middle* by writing on birch-bark slices – the birch tree being an iconic symbol of Ontario. This is depicted in Figure 4.4. For these educators, what mattered most was "getting back to that reflective piece" of "asking effective questions to push your thinking". These slices had statements on them such as "growth: a ripple effect", and "because it grows out from the middle".

Figure 4.4 Leadership From the Middle as Depicted in the Birch-Bark Slices Activity of One District

Leadership From the Middle was experienced by educators not as a mechanistic or bureaucratic phenomenon. Rather, it was an organic activity that "grows and spreads from an idea". It involves "teacher-student voice" and trust to "let it grow, let it flourish".

A Structure of Interdisciplinary Teams

Some educators in the consortium regarded *Leadership From the Middle* as a theory of leadership that entailed placing people "in learning teams and supporting them through their inquiries". "When I think of *Leading From the Middle*", the Superintendent of Leadership and Learning in one district said, "an organization has to put some structures in place and identify what the function of that structure is". In her district, consultants and coaches worked with teachers to improve mathematics learning. In another district, a Mathematics Task Force distributed surveys to ask students what they liked about mathematics, what they found frustrating and difficult, and what kinds of supports they themselves would most like to receive.

Even though these kinds of transformations involved reorganization and information gathering by the educational bureaucracy, there was more to this than simply operating as an intermediary middle tier that implements government policies from the top down. Recalling one of the seven principles of *Leadership From the Middle* in which district personnel take initiative rather than just implementing other people's initiatives, one superintendent observed: "I don't see *Leading From the Middle* as the ministry is at the top and districts are in the middle, and schools are at the bottom. I see that the ministry lays out the game plan for everybody, but the action orientation rests with the districts."[19]

From this point of view, diverse individuals at different levels can *Lead From the Middle*. One director stated that these included "district staff", "system leaders", "school leaders", and others as well. In a district with a high number of students with Foetal Alcohol Spectrum Disorder, for example, mental health professionals provided by community-based non-profit agencies were included as an absolute necessity.

Ontario's educators saw *Leadership From the Middle* as activating everyone in their schools and systems by redesigning the structures of interdisciplinary teams to be diverse and locally responsive. One school principal stated that *Leadership From the Middle* was the "expertise that comes in and helps our team to problem solve. And it helps to build our knowledge and capacity and mindset". For a district director, *Leadership From the Middle* "means advocacy; it means people influencing the direction of the organization from the inside, in the grassroots, as opposed to top-down". *Leadership From the Middle* did not mean building up another bureaucracy with excessive guidelines and constraints, least of all one that was insulated from legitimate public concerns. Rather, it meant "flattening the organization, so it's more that we're all *Leading From the Middle*. We're taking away the hierarchy and protocols and leading all together from the middle. We're all sitting at a table here. You have a voice at the table". With *Leadership From the Middle*, interdisciplinary teams were designed to be responsive, inclusive, and participatory for all.

A Culture of Collaborative Professionalism

Consortium districts experimented with *Leadership From the Middle* not just as a philosophy or a structure, but also as a method of group work. One principal stated that "there is a negative aspect when people are feeling from above them that they're being held back or there are constraints". Instead, as a superintendent noted: "Our *Leading From the Middle* methodology is about the circle as a resolution." "The circle itself is very much an asset-oriented stance" to promote dialogue. "It's about the fact that everybody came [to one meeting] with a little cheat sheet of a few things they wanted to say, but when it comes together, it actually becomes the conversation." These conversations "speak to how *Leading From the Middle* is a whole idea of trust. I'm trusting you to know what's really important for your students, for your staff". A Superintendent of Special Education echoed this view: "I've always believed that *Leadership From the Middle* is all inclusive."

> Somebody raised a point [at a consortium meeting] and said we need to start thinking about our teachers and how they are leaders from the middle as well and it just made me really think differently about the whole concept. It shifted my paradigm a little bit. I thought "She's right!" We have to have that voice. That voice has to be heard! Teachers are an important voice in the *Leading From the Middle* concept.

Eventually, *Leadership From the Middle* overlapped with what Michael O'Connor and I term a *culture of collaborative professionalism* where educators work together for all students' success and well-being in ways that are assertive and show initiative.[20] One district, for example, offered modest amounts of funding up to $1,000 for teachers to undertake innovations together. "I'm trusting you to know what's really important for your students. You have a great idea. Let's see what we can do with it. Let's see how we can make it grow", an administrator said. "They feel connected, they feel comfortable to try something that's specific to their school culture that might be an initiative that might take off and have lift to it", a superintendent added. "Sometimes", a colleague went on, "it starts off locally, and it just spreads from one school to another school, and part of the grant is that idea of sharing so that we can all take it and rework it to fit our own communities". In other words, knowledge is distributed rapidly across schools to enhance teachers' creativity and professionalism:

> At the end of the innovation grants, we come in and we share them. We share them with superintendents, we share them with the director, so people have an idea. We share them with other administrators and various contacts throughout the district, so you'll get people saying, "Oh you did that as innovation grant? That's great. Can we meet? Can I set you up with some teachers?" The teachers who are coming forward are coming forward knowing that they might be asked to be a leader to lead this initiative going forward.

In these cases, the grants for projects funded by teacher unions in collaboration with the ministry for teacher-initiated innovations from the bottom up, began to be circulated by schools among each other in the middle. *Leadership From the Middle*, in this respect, embraced a *culture of collaborative professionalism* – of sharing, initiative, and responsiveness to the needs of the students, educators, and communities in Ontario's schools. This entailed new ways of doing things together and acting independently of top-down control. The *culture* was founded on a *philosophy* that prioritizes democracy and community and that was made possible by clear *structural* design decisions that, together, kept pushing learning and teaching forward with an ethic of care for all students.

Conclusion

If we want inclusion, equity, and success on a considerable scale, this cannot be achieved if districts continue to act independently of one another or if they only work together on limited issues. *Leading From the Middle* can use the power of local solutions to diverse problems in an environment where schools work with schools and where districts collaborate with districts, as they exercise collective initiative and responsibility for all students' success. This approach releases the power of what the Jesuit religious order, political science specialists, and Article 5 (3) of *The Treaty of the European Union* call *subsidiarity*. The Cambridge dictionary defines subsidiarity as "the principle that decisions should always be taken at the lowest possible level or closest to where they will have their effect, for example in a local area rather than a whole country". The subsidiarity of *Leadership From the Middle* brings leadership closer to the heart, soul, and backbone of the work of schools across the diverse and different lands that make up a society.

This kind of leadership needn't be confined to districts and can encompass networks and other kinds of partnerships as well, as we shall see shortly. But collective responsibility is not just something districts should ask others to undertake. Districts must now take this on themselves. This calls for new ways of carrying out policy and change, at the top and bottom as well as in the middle. It also suggests and perhaps even demands new metaphors for *Leadership From the Middle*, that are different from the metaphors that guide too much thinking about *Leading In the Middle*, and about educational policy and change in general. I will unpack these differences of approach and metaphorical understanding between *Leadership From and In the Middle*, and their strategic implications, in the next chapter.

5

AROUND AND ABOUT
THE MIDDLE

Introduction

Our first phase of work in Ontario surfaced the idea of *Leading From the Middle* to us. It then brought *Leadership From the Middle* to the attention of other educational systems. From 2014, the second stage of our work then revealed how *Leadership From the Middle* had become embedded in the thinking and strategies of district leaders in the consortium with whom we collaborated. During this period, we also became aware of how other systems, thought leaders, and policy groups were starting to turn to leading from or in the middle as ways to advance system change. But as we looked at these other examples, we began to discern significant differences between what many of them and us were arguing.

This chapter compares *Leadership From the Middle* and *Leading In the Middle* so that leaders in every part of a school system can be clear about the strategy they are adopting and why. This will avoid ambiguity, confusion, and even deception regarding strategies that fall under the broad and potentially misleading headings and directions of middle level, middle tier, or simply middle leadership. We will learn that Leading *From* rather than *In* the Middle involves not just a tactical shift but a new way of thinking about leadership and education in our schools. This fresh mindset employs new metaphors for educational work and those who lead it. It sets aside mechanical and stereotypically male vocabularies of leadership and change associated with *Leading In the Middle* that destroy the power and possibilities of local

DOI: 10.4324/9781315682921-5

communities. These are replaced with more organic and sustainable ways of thinking and being, in which many female political leaders especially seem to excel.[1]

The chapter concludes by examining what *Leadership From the Middle* requires of the leadership that we still think of as occurring at the top and bottom of a system. It also documents how this work is influencing and being influenced by other systems elsewhere. In other words, this chapter is about the distinctive identity of *Leadership From the Middle* versus *Leading In the Middle*, and it looks around at what *Leadership From the Middle* means for the (so-called) top and bottom of a school system, and for other systems beyond.

Leading *From*, Not *In* the Middle

Leadership From the Middle strategies within Ontario brought about inclusive education reform. Initially, they focused on developing all students' achievement and success, especially among students who were most vulnerable, by taking collective responsibility for measurable improvements in these students' learning results. After *Achieving Excellence* in 2014, with its emphasis on broad excellence, well-being, and equity understood as inclusion, school and system leaders started to view *Leadership From the Middle* as a strategy to help them move closer to *all* their students and support their learning and development. *Leadership From the Middle* now addressed genuine concerns for all students, and it built authentic collaboration with other educators to achieve this end. *Leadership From the Middle* was not just about middle-level implementation, like *Leading In the Middle*. The differences between the two approaches are summarized in Table 5.1.

Table 5.1 Contrasting Roles of the Middle in System Leadership

Leading In the Middle	*Leading From the Middle*
Level, layer, or tier	Centre, core, and heart
Improving performance	Transforming learning and well-being
Better systems	Stronger communities
Coherence and connection	Collective responsibility
Implementing initiatives	Taking initiative

In market systems, or systems focused on narrowly defined priorities such as literacy and mathematics, *Leading In the Middle* has been about increasing achievement scores in line with top-down priorities. *Leading In the Middle* bypasses or replaces local democracy in a push to partly privatize schools or impose top-down mandates.

Leading From the Middle is not against stronger performance or improved coherence. But it approaches them differently. It is inclusive and empowering, and it engages with people through all parts of the school system. In this way, *Leadership From the Middle* strengthens local communities and local responsibility rather than just increasing the efficiency of the larger system.

Leadership From the Middle, then, regards those in the middle not just as a mediating layer or tier that connects the bottom to the top, but as encouraging and addressing the heart and soul of leadership at its core. *Leadership From the Middle* is about much more than making incremental adjustments among levels to raise performance or about developing more coherent systems that fit together effectively. It is about the subsidiarity of supporting educators who are closest to the work of teaching and learning in classrooms and schools so they can collaborate purposefully, responsibly, and transparently. It is about local, collective authority, expertise, and confidence to develop new strategies to educate the children educators work with every day. This involves thinking about what the middle is and what it involves in a completely different way.

Metaphors of the Middle

How people lead or change organizations is related to the metaphors they use to understand them. In the title of their defining book on the subject, George Lakoff and Mark Johnson called them *Metaphors We Live By*.[2] People use metaphors to inspire others, to explain the need for change to them, and to justify their own approach. Metaphors lend meaning and intensity to our work and our mental and emotional lives. They shape and guide our thinking and the ways we interact with other people.

We use metaphors all the time. Perhaps we may describe a great leader as a legend. An exciting but chaotic project is often termed a bit of a rollercoaster. A bold, ambitious, and risky undertaking is a moonshot. Opposition to change is described as resistance. A negative school culture may be toxic. We talk about career ladders and windows of opportunity. We may also describe ourselves as in a hole if things are going badly. Metaphors are everywhere. We can't avoid them. The point is not whether we should use metaphors or not. It's a question of which ones we choose.

We use clusters of metaphors to describe the actual or anticipated course of our work and lives, including the things we lead. As a passionate hiker of long-distance trails, I often find myself drawn to the overarching metaphor of a journey. This is one of the most ancient metaphors of all – the Odyssey, the quest, and the pilgrimage, for example. This journey may present different paths or ways forward – hence my coauthored books with Dennis Shirley on *The Fourth Way* of educational change.[3] Fellow travellers and I may encounter many obstacles along the way – an issue I addressed earlier in terms of rethinking how obstacles might turn out to be the way all along. Distractions can take us off course, but great rewards await those who stay true to the cause and stay on course.

For decades now, one of the most common sets of metaphors in policy making and leadership in Western nations has been associated with a mechanical or industrial world of buildings, construction, engineering design, and transportation. It's a hyper-masculine world of machines and automobiles. We use a *toolbox* of strategies when we are dealing with a change. If we want good ideas to reach more people, we *scale* them up, from a tiny prototype into a vast edifice. We *build* capacity. We look for the best *levers* for change. Policies and practices must be in *alignment* and results get measured as *outputs*, like industrial or agricultural production rates. Knowledge is *mobilized* as if it were a container ship or an army. We identify the *drivers* of change as if they were in an automobile. Our ideas are listed in *bullet* points. And when we promise to make change happen, we talk about *delivering* it, as if it arrived on a truck or in a van. There's even a policy-making approach called *deliverology* that several governments have adopted.[4]

Leading In the Middle – the kind of leadership that enables policy makers to achieve their outcomes without local interference – uses a vocabulary of construction that entails tops, bottoms, levels, and tiers.

It's an abstract and systemic language. It takes all the human meaning out of educational and organizational change that Michael Fullan established as being immensely important in the 1980s.[5]

In 2016, in one of his last books – *Creative Schools: The Grassroots Revolution that's Transforming Education* – the late Sir Ken Robinson argued that we need to ditch outdated and insensitive metaphors for schools that have been guided by industrial and large-scale agricultural production, and adopt more nature-based, organic metaphors that are more suited to learning and children.[6]

In a videocast for the ARC Education Collaboratory, Sir Ken described what a more organic language of education and schools and of the "sustainable and natural processes" in them involves and achieves. "Organic farmers promote diversity", he said, not standardized monocultures of large-scale production. "They look at the health and ecology of the whole system." "We've lost sight of the natural processes of teaching and learning", he continued, and with it, the "culture of education" and learning. "It's time to change the metaphor", he insisted, and see "education as a human process in which children flourish under certain sorts of conditions" in the right kind of school climate. Not only is it "our job is to create those conditions in schools", it's also the job of "districts and of nations to create an overall political climate where those things are encouraged" to "make the most of our natural resources": children, teachers, and learning.[7]

Leadership From the Middle embraces and advances this metaphor. Children grow and develop. They don't merely perform and produce. They are not gaps to be narrowed nor benchmarks to be met. Like the birch bark branches that district leaders described in the last chapter, the system grows and develops too – like rings on a tree, and interlocking roots in a forest, spreading out from the centre. To mix the metaphor only slightly, in a biological sense, *Leadership From the Middle* gets to the heart of everything, as in someone's body or at the centre of the rings that mark the year-by-year life and growth of a tree. *Leadership From the Middle* is also the backbone of a system that holds it together. It is a living process that needs nourishment and room to breathe if it and all the people it serves are to flourish. It's not a hierarchy of standardized and homogeneous levels in a mechanical system of engineering design. As we will see in the next chapter, it is a network of diverse elements that cross-fertilize each other and make the environment rich and resilient. It's a healthy system that nourishes healthy children. It's not mechanical. It's sustainable.

In saying all this, neither Ken Robinson nor I are suggesting that we should flee from modern society and return to some original state of nature. This is as naïve as thinking that enjoyment of the outdoors should involve escaping from civilization into pristine wilderness. We are all part of nature and vice versa. The moment we step into a wilderness, it's not a wilderness anymore, because we are now in it. Even when environmentalist Henry David Thoreau retreated into his cabin, he still had his mother do his laundry for him! And when we enjoy the outdoors, there is nothing wrong with doing this in European rather than North American style – finding a room at night in a local inn and supporting local communities and economies as we do so instead of camping as far away from humanity as is possible. Similarly, looking at schools and school systems in an organic and sustainable way is not about retreating to nature and the innocence of children in the face of a corrupted civilization. It is about learning from nature and living with nature, and with each other, as an essential part of who we are.

In a world where climate change is one of the Big Five omni-crises that are threatening us, adopting an organic and environmentally sustainable metaphor of learning and leadership is not romantic. It is radical and realistic.

In 2022, one of the twentieth century's most remarkable and influential thinkers, James Lovelock, passed away at the age of 103.[8] This scientist, philosopher, and activist changed the way we think, or at least should think, about our relationship with our planet. In doing so, he helped to initiate the sustainability movement. Lovelock was best known for his Gaia theory: a controversial idea he proposed in the 1960s that looked at the evolution of life very differently compared to modern science at the time. Gaia held that the countless trillions of organisms not only competed, but also cooperated to maintain an environment in which life could be sustained: a process of co-evolution. As indigenous peoples have understood for eons, the fates of people and the planet are indivisible. In 2001, more than 1,000 scientists met in Amsterdam to declare that the planet "behaves as a single, self-regulating system comprised of physical, chemical, biological and human components".[9] Mocked and ostracized throughout his career, Lovelock proved to be right all along. He was not a romantic, but a radical, and also a realist that our perilous times had been waiting for.

Leadership From the Middle is related to and expresses the essential elements of this environmental philosophy. In 2006, Dean Fink and I argued that *Sustainable Leadership* and change "preserves and develops deep learning for all that spreads and lasts, in ways that do no harm to and indeed create positive benefits for others now and in the future".[10] One of the book's seven principles was and is diversity. Sustainable leadership, it argued, "promotes cohesive diversity; it fosters and learns from diversity and creates cohesion and networking among its richly varying components".[11] Strong natural systems are bio-diverse rather than standardized and homogeneous. So are strong organizations that promote the cross-pollination of learning, ideas, and of the capacity within a system and its diverse, local resources to bounce back and recover quickly in the face of adversity.

Leadership From the Middle is not about stacking up levels of implementation (another mechanical metaphor in which implements are tools) – that is merely *Leading In the Middle*. It is about being able to respond to and nurture interconnected local diversities of culture, race, religion, identity, and economies. It is about a whole ecosystem supporting whole schools that serve the whole child, in rich cultures and networked relationships of collaboration for every young person's learning and well-being.

In Greek mythology, the Goddess Gaia was preceded by Chaos. The excessive pursuit of industrial and agricultural growth and production in which growth-obsessed economies have been forever conquering and then obliterating nature have left us with the Big Five chaos that confronts us today. Likewise, decades of obsession with standardized practices to deliver national performance numbers that meet educational and economic production targets in never-ending and unsustainable races to the top, have been destroying the health, well-being, and learning of our young people and their communities too. The push to eliminate local community democracies that impede government drives for constant growth, higher standards, and mechanical races to the top is part of this unnatural way of leading, as is the move to replace these lost local democracies with abstract, intermediary levels of implementation.

Looking at leadership, including and especially *Leadership From the Middle*, in more organic and sustainable terms encourages us all to foster diversity and thrive on it and to renew rather than deplete people's energy by staying close to the beating heart of learning, children, and their education. This means paying more attention to the middle. It also means fundamentally rethinking what the middle means. Last, but by no means least, thinking organically and sustainably means repositioning the role of leadership and change from what we've previously thought of as being the top and the bottom of the system to something or somewhere else too.

Above and Beneath

If we must rethink what it means to have *Leadership From the Middle*, we can't avoid confronting long-standing assumptions and traditions of top-down and bottom-up change and leadership either. For this, we need to persevere for a bit longer with our organic and biological metaphors – though we must also avoid overdoing them. All metaphors have their limits and can be overstretched. Ones that are organic and biological are no exception. The nineteenth-century British social theorist, Herbert Spencer, for example, attracted acclaim for his interpretation of society through a biological analogy of interdependent, functionally related body parts, but he also drew criticism for likening every bodily organ and their functions to parts of the social system.[12]

So, let's explore the metaphor a bit further, but keep its limitations in mind. When we look at leadership in and by governments, we tend to think of it as the top of a hierarchy of decision-making, like office blocks where the executive suites are on the highest floor, overseeing everything and everyone else. Top-down change is passed down from above to be implemented faithfully underneath within a hierarchy of compliance. As we saw in Chapter 2, top-down change can be cynical or benign, but even at its best, it tends to work well only when systems and system reforms have a mechanical simplicity to them.

Supposing, though, that we regard what's on top more like the head on a body: be it bureaucratic or corporate in nature. This head does much of the strategic thinking for the organization. It doesn't do it alone, but it can see far into the distance and have some vision of what may be on the horizon. In a way, the head is the body's executive function. It carries out a lot of its thinking and planning. Its positioning above everyone else in a biological sense does not lend it more hierarchical importance, though. And it certainly gives it no right to pass down mandates based on what it can sometimes see more readily. The head of a school is like the British word for school principal: *headteacher*. It belongs to and serves the organization like everyone else. It's still essentially a teacher but just now the head of all the teachers – helping the school think about what to do and where to go next.

Beneath the head are the feet and the hands. Feet matter. Soldiers with trench foot lose their ability to fight. Seniors whose mobility in their feet deteriorates lose balance and agility in their minds as well as their bodies. Our feet give us something to stand on. They move us forward. They keep us grounded. And they let us and everyone else sense when something is afoot or about to happen.

According to the Merriam-Webster dictionary, bottom-up change is a management term where change is "progressing upward from the lowest levels (as of a stratified organization or system)".[13] It is a not especially flattering way to characterize people at the lowest levels of a system's hierarchy who are trying to instigate change. In the Cambridge dictionary, bottom-up leadership and change is even less worthy. It is about "considering the smaller or less important parts or details of a plan, organization, etc. first".[14]

Heads and feet are not upper and lower levels – tops and bottoms in hierarchies of power and control. They are essential and integral parts of living and breathing organic systems. The educators who work in the classrooms of our nations are not a bottom layer or tier. They give leaders something of character to stand on. They keep schools grounded, especially in the face of lofty thinking that may be oblivious to day-to-day realities. Assign more decisions to everyday educators and they will be more nimble, agile, and locally grounded than people at the head of the organization when a disruption, a crisis, or an opportunity comes along.

When I hike through the endless forests of America's Appalachian Trail at a very brisk pace that comes close to trail running, my head and feet must always be perfectly in synch with each other as I bound along the rocky footways of my journey. Let my mind wander or miss my footing for one second, and I can find myself in serious jeopardy, as I did when I broke my ankle in 2018 and had to be carried down the mountain at night by more than a dozen members of the New Hampshire Fish and Game Commission. The head and feet are not separate. They must work together, in close coordination, as if they were one. The same principle applies in our schools and other organizations if we think of them in organic and natural rather than hierarchical and systemic terms.

If we separate people at the head of a school, of another organization, or of an entire society, from people at the foot of it, we are going to get into trouble. One person who understood this was the legendary 1920s German silent film director, Fritz Lang. Lang's epic movie, *Metropolis*, was restored in 2010 when I was able to view it in the Filmmuseum in Berlin.[15] *Metropolis* portrays a rigid and cruel class society where a wealthy creative elite at its head oppresses a labouring underclass beneath it. This is a familiar enough refrain – from Aldous Huxley's *Brave New World* and George Orwell's *1984*, to the award-winning movie series, *The Hunger Games,* and the children's animated movie *The Sea Beast*.[16] What is different about *Metropolis* is that the injustice of a brutal and extreme class system is not resolved by individual escape or by collective insurrection but by a mediator, who serves as the heart that unites the hands and the head. "The mediator between head and hands must be the heart!", asserts one of the movie's protagonists.[17]

Metropolis could have been about the feet as much as the hands. Handmaidens and foot soldiers alike all implement higher orders and are undervalued and even devalued in both cases. Feeling, thinking, and doing must not be separated out but brought together in individuals and in communities. A unity between thought, emotion, and practice is an organic one and it is integral to humanistic conceptions of learning as well as leadership. The eighteenth-century Swiss educator, Johann Heinrich Pestalozzi, a founding theorist of child pedagogy, established four institutes where he sought to promote children's development, happiness, and well-being through a trinity "with the head, heart and hands".[18] All students were engaged in intellectual and manual work. They took learning walks together outdoors. Attention was paid to their moral and spiritual development along with education in the conventional subjects of the school curriculum.

Head, heart, and hand are at the core of the whole child's development. They are integral to indigenous knowledge wheels of learning and leadership.[19] They unite people with nature. They are organically interrelated and promote a sustainable quality of life in a more sustainable world. This is how we need to see leadership too; not as a disconnect or separation between top and bottom, in a mechanical hierarchy of implementation, where intermediary levels are meant to get an outdated and unsustainable system to work more efficiently. Rather, we should see head, hands (and feet), and heart working together, uniting thought, passion, and practice. Whether it's the metaphor of an embodied person, of interconnected birch bark branches, or of organically integrated and environmentally sustainable societies, *Leadership From the Middle* involves a different way of thinking not just about the middle, but about so-called top-down and bottom-up change too.

The head shows everyone where to go. The feet get us there and keep us upright. And the heart makes us want to set off in the first place. The challenge for the heads of systems contemplating some version or other of *Leading From the Middle* is to inspire, guide and steer everyone in the right direction, and shift more resources from the centre of the ministry to the districts and to affiliated professional organizations with successful track records of initiating and spreading change. A system can't *Lead From the Middle* haphazardly or temporarily. It must be organized to *Lead From the Middle* sustainably.

It's time to change the metaphor and time to change the game of *Leadership From the Middle* in education. Learning aspirations must be directed at improving quality of life for everyone, in a world where we must not only adapt to the Big Five omni-crisis, but ultimately overcome it. This needs leadership of the many, not just the few. And this must include our students: the leaders of tomorrow.

Beside and Beyond

Ontario has not been alone in its efforts to lead from the middle across districts. Through the work my colleagues and I have undertaken with the province and its consortium of districts, we have reached out to learn from and lend a helping hand to other systems that seek an improved quality of life for all their students and for their societies.

Around the same time that ESGA was gathering steam, England was making various efforts to improve quality and equity by getting districts to work together. One of these was *the Greater Manchester Challenge (GMC)*. The GMC was initiated in 2007–8 by the government. It brought together ten school districts (known in England as local authorities) to improve standards over three years. Professor Mel Ainscow, an international expert on inclusion, was appointed as senior adviser to this US$80 million project. Given his years of researching and advocating for educational equity and inclusion, and his attachments to the area because he had been educated there as a child, Ainscow was very motivated to accept this full-time position to promote system-wide equity and improvement. His heart was in it. When the project was announced, he stated publicly that "There are lots of good things going on in schools in Greater Manchester. The task now is to spread the best practice to all schools."[20] But how would this be done?

- Leaders of successful schools worked with weaker schools across the districts to improve their leadership teams.
- Schools with similar student populations were clustered to share best practices.
- Local problems would be met with local solutions.

Getting schools to collaborate was not a new phenomenon in England. But while previous school-to-school networks and partnerships had tended to take place within local authorities (school districts) or to bypass local authorities altogether through networks that transcended them, ten neighbouring local authorities would now be driving improvement together. In the words of a planning committee member, "This is simple. The job of schools is to improve themselves. Our job is to make sure this happens."[21]

Multiple strategies brought this principle to life. Many of these involved schools cooperating across local authority boundaries. Recently turned around schools became the "keys to success" in helping other schools. Hub schools that demonstrated excellence in particular areas provided extensive training and development for teachers in other schools and local authorities. Schools at different stages of development were organized in "families". A Jewish school assisted a predominantly Muslim partner. A Catholic school prayed for a good inspection result for its secular counterpart. Hidden capacity was capitalized on, knowledge was moved around, and old rivalries were overcome in pursuit of the higher purpose of the whole area's regeneration.

The Manchester area had suffered from problems of unemployment and deprivation for four decades, but by 2011, its schools were above the national average on all indicators of success. Secondary schools in the most disadvantaged communities improved at three times the rate of the national average. By working together, school leaders changed the cultures of the schools. Instead of blaming parents in poor families for not being interested in their children's learning, schools came to appreciate the great stresses these families were under and then responded with local flexibility and intensive support. There was a focus on better, more interesting teaching and learning, through strategies like cooperative learning and Lesson Study. There was pressure on teachers and schools to work hard to improve results, but also more emphasis on caring for the adults in the schools as well as the children, so that the schools became happy and professionally fulfilling places to work.

None of this was easy. Local authorities in England are political entities as well as providers of services. Internal conflicts and external turf wars were often exacerbated by national policies that promoted inter-school competition. A Steering Committee involving national government and local representatives got locked into conflicts over the budget. A committee of leaders of the ten authorities became fractious whenever it was presented with disturbing data or with concerns about lack of progress. While six of the authorities were willing to change roles and responsibilities, two others accommodated the new language of shared responsibility for improvement without making any real changes in practice. But over time, with persistence, relationships improved, some personnel changed, and ideas and strategies started to be shared among schools as well as within them.

The impact of the GMC inspired other systems to adopt similar strategies. For example, in neighbouring Wales, a 2013 OECD review team to which I contributed recommended that there should be a national initiative to get schools across the country's 22 strong but very independent local authorities to work more closely and effectively together.[22] By sharing expertise among schools, between schools and their local communities, and between national and local government, the programme demonstrated early gains and continued to show improvement through cross-district collaboration following further support from Ainscow and others.[23]

Likewise, in *Scotland*, following another country review by the OECD in 2015 to which I also contributed, principles of *Leadership From the Middle* were recommended to get the 32 local authorities to work together in six Regional Improvement Collaboratives (RICs).[24] The RICs share resources and ideas and take collective responsibility for improved equity and for reducing variation of quality across districts. Each RIC is also assigned a challenge adviser to push and support it to keep improving with relentless determination. The RICs contributed to continued improvement in Scotland from 2015 until the COVID-19 pandemic, including some of the most rapid improvements on the OECD's 2017 PISA tests in reading that also exceeded those of any other UK nation.[25]

In too many countries, school districts have been driven to distraction and to near-destruction by top-down changes that have undermined or bypassed their authority and the communities they serve. Our own and others' mounting evidence is that districts have the capability to be a big part of a better future for our children, if they are willing to collaborate to embrace and share changes in their thinking and practice.

Leadership From the Middle has gained less traction in the United States than other parts of the world, however. Neighbouring districts often find themselves in deeply competitive relationships because of extreme gaps of wealth and poverty, trying to recruit the same quality teachers and leaders from a shrinking pool, or serving communities with very different racial or economic demographics.[26] Where collaboration does exist, efforts focus on weaker aspects of sharing like making efficiencies through common use of facilities and resources such as transportation, or on engaging in joint professional learning with take-it-or-leave-it follow-through, based on what may or may not have been learned. There are few examples of districts taking collective responsibility for all students' success.

One exception is California which has undertaken several initiatives in cross-district collaboration. For instance, from 2011 to 2018, 18 (originally 25) small and mainly rural school districts joined a project to stimulate and support school improvement efforts in relation to literacy and mathematics learning.[27] Participants used the meetings to share experiences and insights among their peers, gain access to content experts provided by a coordinating body, and develop and then try to refine and implement their improvement plans. An evaluation of this initiative pointed to self-reported improvements in access to colleagues' ideas and insights, the development of a mindset for continuous improvement, and increased attention to development and implementation of improvement plans.[28] However, perhaps because the project design did not include collective responsibility for shared success, or because the districts were spread out rather than in a shared geographic area, there was no hard evidence of improvements in student achievement, and there were only anecdotal indicators of other positive effects.

From 2010, seven, and later ten, California school districts and their administrators collaborated to implement new academic standards and improve teacher quality.[29] They engaged in professional learning to familiarize themselves with the standards, then designed a common set of 64 related assessment modules. Despite the amount of joint work and the value of focusing on a common product, use of the modules within the districts seemed extremely limited. In effect, this collaboration was about districts implementing someone else's standards designed at the top rather than making change themselves. It was leading *in* rather than *from* the middle. When the districts turned to a more open-ended task of investing in and developing professional capital among educators, agreement and results were even weaker. Districts seemed less able to design products and learn from each other's strategies when the task was more open-ended.

These examples reveal how difficult it is to have *Leadership From the Middle* across US school districts not just because of the competitive relationships among them, but also because of the sheer quantity of top-down mandates and regulations which leave districts mainly focusing on implementation of other people's policies and standards rather than on making policy changes of their own.

In truth, districts across the United States repeatedly come up against huge competition and massive inequalities in relation to their neighbours and in relation to the proliferation of charter schools that have often taken resources, aspiring families, and higher quality teachers and principals from the districts in which they are located. Until the United States and its states are willing to address these savage inequalities head-on, the prospects for deep inter-district collaboration that extends beyond sharing some resources or undergoing a few joint learning exercises together seem slim, at best. In the meantime, the answer may be found in another kind of *Leadership From the Middle* – leading through networks.

Conclusion

The COVID-19 pandemic made many of us realize that after decades of pursuing more wealth and greater growth in our economies and in our performance numbers in education, there was something that mattered more than this – our health. Leaders in democracies who ignored their people's health during the pandemic and put economics and their own self-interest ahead of it, suffered mightily in the ballot box when the next elections came round. In England, Brazil, Australia, the United States, and parts of Canada, governments who acted arbitrarily, secretively, dishonestly, and unpredictably and showed callous disregard for the heath and lives of their citizens paid the price at the next election.

The pandemic woke people up from their materialistic, self-seeking, and consumerist slumbers. Family members and friends sometimes died needlessly. Children were cut off from their friends and teachers, and digital learning proved to be a poor substitute for all they had lost. Edicts from headstrong governments incurred chaos and anxiety on all those who had to respond to them. Collaborative governments who worked in partnership with professionals and health specialists fared much better. Health and well-being were no longer a luxury to be indulged once achievement had been taken care of. They were matters of life and death.

As young people and their families stopped sleepwalking, they became more and more alert to everything that was threatening their very existence. Obscene wealth accumulated by oil and online corporations exposed how everyone else was left scrabbling for what was left. Climate change turned from being a distant abstraction to a real and present danger that destroyed communities and disrupted supply chains. Racism, culture wars, xenophobia, and attempts to engineer totalitarian takeovers of democracies were stoked up to get people scrabbling among each other for what was left. But many people were not fooled at all, and young voters as well as young people in general started to turn to policies and leaders who didn't deny the scale and scope of the world's problems, but who engaged students and others with acknowledging and then trying to solve them.

The purpose of education has started to return to what many countries have left behind for too long – the development of people with character, imagination, and civic responsibility in a society that sees inclusion as the key to equity. The organic metaphor for education and society may prove to be our lifeline. Leaders everywhere must get closer to the heart and soul of young people's learning in this crisis-ridden world, to what will enable them to turn everything around, now and in the years to come, before it's too late. This means avoiding weak forms of *Leading In the Middle* that exist mostly to implement outdated and outworn priorities in tested achievement results without interference from democratically elected local communities. Instead, *Leadership From the Middle* calls for us to embrace the subsidiarity of making decisions among those who will be most affected by them in local, diverse, rapidly changing, and constantly threatened communities that are strengthened through their connections with one another. Doing this across school districts is one way to achieve that end. Developing networks within and beyond those districts – the subject of the next chapter – is another.

6

LEADING NETWORKS FROM THE MIDDLE

with Danette Parsley

The Nature of Networks

Geography isn't always destiny. Schools that are not part of a local district need not be isolated. Even ones that are part of a district do not have to be totally place-bound in their relationships of learning, support, and leadership. Leadership and learning can transcend local geography, reaching out to schools in other regions and even across the world. This is increasingly possible and desirable in a digital age of virtual connections. That is what networks are for.

Networks are not a new idea. Brain circuitry and ecosystems behave like complex networks. Networks came into fashion because they are prominent in the digital world. But organically, they have been around since life began. Today, they are everywhere.

Elites have used networks of old school alumni and family ties to procure and perpetuate privilege. Resistance movements have employed networks to try to undermine or overthrow elites. Criminals and terrorists operate in networks. So do mothers who share knowledge and strategies about raising their kids. Organizations operate as networks of information and communication. This applies to schools and teachers too.

Networks are ways to describe how people already interact with others in organizations, communities, and societies. They also describe deliberate efforts to articulate new interactions among people to support and promote innovation, and implementation of change.

DOI: 10.4324/9781315682921-6

Professional networks and school networks exemplify these deliberately designed architectures. Networks have a range of properties that include:

- *Size*: networks can be large, small, or in between.
- *Density*: dense networks have many interactions out of all those that are statistically possible, which leads to greater cohesion.
- *Centrality*: networks can have all communication going through a central, controlling hub; or highly decentralized with many patterns of interaction that bypass and do not directly involve the hub.
- *Between-ness and closeness*: people in networks may be between only one or two others, or in long chains that connect them to many others.
- *Transitivity*: people connected to you may also be connected to each other to a greater or lesser degree.[1]

There are many different sorts of network structures. UK professors Mark Hadfield and Chris Chapman point to three of them, as illustrated in Figure 6.1:[2]

- *Hub-and-spoke networks* disseminate information from a central hub to participants on the periphery. University relationships with partner schools often take this form.
- *Nodal networks* comprise mini hubs, as in schools that are clustered together by region, level, or focus, to implement and give feedback on government initiatives.
- *Crystalline networks* have few or no recognizable hubs. Interactions across the network occur on multiple and overlapping pathways of communication.

A key issue in networks is whether people have strong or weak ties with each other. Communities typically have strong ties among members where there are close and frequent interactions with high levels of relational or personal trust among necessarily small numbers of participants. But Barry Wellman, one of the foundational theorists

Figure 6.1 Three Kinds of Networks

of networks, and creator of the idea of *networks of networks,* argues that in modern society, weaker ties of less intimate but more numerous interactions are more typical and perhaps even more valuable.[3]

In 1973, Stanford University professor, Mark Granovetter, interviewed 282 workers in the Boston area about how they acquired their jobs. In 84 per cent of cases, the jobs were attained through someone they knew, but this was usually a casual acquaintance rather than a close friend. Weak ties such as these are an underestimated aspect of community life, Granovetter argued. The person who delivers your mail, the neighbour who walks their dog past your home, or the colleague you exchange ideas with but do not meet socially – these kinds of ties and associations hold people together and help organizations develop the cooperation that gets things done.[4]

In 1990, Berkeley University professor, Judith Warren Little, argued that weak ties are also important in schools.[5] Weak ties enable professional work to be completed by people who can focus on tasks together without the prerequisites of strong friendship or without the close interactions that stronger ties presume. Weak ties lead not only to greater productivity but also to greater well-being and happiness, wrote Ian Leslie for the BBC in 2020.[6] This, he went on, was one of the most important aspects of social and workplace cohesion that lockdown during the COVID-19 pandemic took away from people. Indeed, one striking initiative to reverse this process occurred in Ireland where postal workers organized themselves to check up on the health and welfare of vulnerable people in lockdown to whom they already regularly delivered letters and packages.[7]

Purposes of Networks

Traditionally, educational change has been approached through the ideas of implementing policy or utilizing knowledge. Policy implemented from the top has historically been impeded by countless obstacles such as insufficient funding, lack of training, poor resources, insufficient time to understand and interpret new mandates, ineffective leadership, lack of clarity, inconsistent interpretation by disconnected teachers, and, not least, resistance to the purpose and intent of the policy itself. Knowledge utilization or dissemination – the practice of trying to move research-based knowledge into people's practice – has been beset with similar problems.

University of Minnesota professor, Karen Seashore Louis, has spent much of her career studying how knowledge about successful classroom practice and effective change strategies can be used and disseminated. Traditional ways of thinking about these processes through knowledge utilization theory, she argues, address how knowledge is produced and then disseminated. What matters is not so much "where the knowledge comes from", or even "the linkage mechanism" to practice, Louis wrote in 2005, but rather "the structures and culture that will encourage the development of a shared knowledge base that will guide collective action".[8] One condition of successful knowledge use is "sustained interactivity" between developers and users within "formal and informal networks . . . that combine research knowledge and practice knowledge".[9]

Ten years later, Louis added that effective utilization depended on sustained interaction and collaborative cultures where teachers could learn about and make sense of changes together.[10] She also highlighted the importance of networks as mechanisms for diffusing innovations that resonated with practitioners among mixed groups of researchers, educators, and policy makers. At their best, networks spread new ideas and sustain commitment to them. They don't disseminate or even mobilize knowledge. They *circulate* knowledge and move it around.

Networks are not especially new in education, though. Teachers College Columbia professor, Tom Hatch, refers to several that he has been involved with throughout his career. These include the *Coalition for Essential Schools* network committed to nine basic principles of school design, the *(James) Comer Schools* that connected schools to their communities, the *Alliance Schools* in Texas that pioneered community organizing in education, and the *New Jersey Network of Superintendents* who tried to improve their schools using "instructional rounds" of classroom observation.[11] There have been many other networks over the years within the United States alone, such as the national Critical Friends group of teachers that has clear protocols to give each other mutual feedback, the National Writing Project that Ann Lieberman and Diane Wood researched and supported, and the more than 275 Big Picture Schools that have promoted student-centred learning in the United States and across the world.[12]

Networks used to be and often still are outlier structures for outlier schools and teachers – ways to gather eccentric or innovative schools and teachers together into one loosely structured oddball organization outside the mainstream. But in the twenty-first century, networks have also become more integral to state policy, have sometimes provided a significant alternative to it, and have even evolved into a parallel form of large-scale organizational change altogether, in some cases.

Networks have expanded almost exponentially in the information age. Digital technology has increased and expanded communication and communication networks in what Catalan social theorist, Manuel Castells, anticipated was becoming a "network society" even by the 1990s.[13] Not all networks are positive, of course. Like many other phenomena, they also have a dark side. For instance, in education, high-status parents can resist interdisciplinary or other changes that threaten their interests by organizing through networks. Evangelical and fundamentalist parents of many faiths can also be roused up and mobilized to ban textbooks that contain elements and identities that offend their beliefs.[14]

In the first quarter of the twenty-first century, networks have gained increasing traction and popularity in response to two developments. First, educational goals have become deeper and more sophisticated to encompass competencies that extend far beyond the basics of literacy, mathematics, and science achievement as measured by standardized test scores or high school examination results. Top-down implementation struggles to secure the understanding and motivation among educators that is necessary to make these goals achievable. Second, declining faith in local community control and the growth of educational markets and market competition among schools have weakened the traditional middle that local school districts used to occupy. Networks of various kinds have come to be seen as a new middle that can achieve broader goals by building professional commitment and by spreading around knowledge of how to make change happen.

Today, networks may be constructed by state agencies to assist implementation efforts, they can arise from voluntary initiatives among teachers or schools, or they can emerge from investments by philanthropies, not-for-profits, or private companies who want to recruit schools to networks that advance learning or well-being as well as their own brand. These networks can serve large numbers of students, teachers, and schools, and sometimes encompass whole systems. Networks are no longer eccentric exceptions to traditionally run state systems. They are substantial, fluid, and flexible systems involving various degrees of self-organizing in and of themselves.

Networks, then, have increasingly come to be seen as ways to implement policy, improve practice, undertake innovation, and create community and system coherence that is different from traditional top-down policy alignment. With the right resources and supports, professional networks offer a promising but by no means guaranteed strategy to help schools and teachers who experience considerable isolation and find themselves physically distanced from easily available assistance.

I have been involved in co-designing, evaluating, and offering advice on educational networks in Canada, the United States, United Kingdom, and Australia since the early 2000s.[15] Drawing on this research-informed experience and on the existing and rapidly expanding literature on educational networks, the rest of this chapter discusses and analyses two different kinds of educational networks, then concludes with some guidelines about what it is important to consider when designing one's own network:

- improvement networks
- innovation networks

The chapter excludes a third kind of network – implementation networks – since these are typically hub-and-spoke operations that establish local clusters of schools, leaders, or teachers, to implement government priorities. At best, they are forms of leading in and not from the middle, mainly to get policies delivered properly.

Improvement Networks

While innovation is focused on introducing new ideas and practices, improvement is about solving problems, and increasing efficiency and expertise. This is in line with Hatch's incremental adjustments that increase quality and outcomes in existing practice. Improvement networks connect schools at different levels of performance to provide mentoring, technical assistance, and support for ones that appear to be struggling.

School-to-school collaboration for improvement first emerged on a considerable scale in England during the period when Tony Blair was prime minister. It was designed to raise levels of performance and effectiveness and to assist struggling schools. I was involved in three of these efforts.

Around 2008–11, when Alma Harris, Alan Boyle, and I were conducting a project on unusually high-performing organizations, we undertook a case study of the London borough of Tower Hamlets.[16] It was using school-to-school collaboration as a key component of an integrated array of strategies to lift performance in its disadvantaged community. Tower Hamlets had high rates of unemployment, more than 50 per cent of families were first-generation immigrants from Bangladesh, and there were more children on free school meals than almost anywhere else in the country. In ten years, between 1997 and 2007, Tower Hamlets transformed from being England's lowest performing school district (local authority) to achieving above the national average. Under visionary leadership and alongside efforts to recruit and retain higher quality teachers, and to involve community members in the life and work of the schools, Tower Hamlets brought schools together to meet shared and ambitious achievement targets that they set for themselves, and to rally round and assist schools that had fallen into official categories of being "failing" schools.

Five years after Tower Hamlet's decade-long rise, the neighbouring borough of Hackney had replaced it as the country's worst performing local authority.[17] But, by 2012, it had also made striking progress in educational achievement. Schools collaborated even more closely and systematically than in Tower Hamlets. For instance, students who were especially challenging, particularly in relation to their behaviour, were assigned to other schools collectively, as a shared responsibility, based on what was best for the student and not just convenient for the school. Schools were also organized into federations – a strategy that was gaining more widespread adoption throughout the country – where the principal (headteacher) who had successfully transformed one school would then take another school and even another under their wing to help transform them also – while building leadership behind them so that their original schools did not suffer as a result. Even in a competitive system of school choice, all schools in Hackney improved, results rose above the national average, more and more graduating students went to Oxford and Cambridge, and instead of parents fleeing the authority to take their children to other schools, students started to move into Hackney schools from neighbouring districts.

In the early 2000s, the *Specialist Schools and Academies Trust* in England – an organization that administered and coordinated most secondary schools – established the *Raising Achievement, Transforming Learning Network* (RATL).[18] The purpose of the network was to improve achievement results in 300 underperforming secondary schools. Counterintuitively, these schools were networked with each other with the idea that they would provide mutual support and realize that low performance was not a matter of their own individual shame but was a problem shared by many schools that called for collective responsibility among them. The 300 schools were paired with self-chosen higher-performing mentor schools to access guidance and expertise. They were also provided with menus of effective practical strategies that would lead to rapid improvement. With Dennis Shirley, Corrie Stone Johnson, and Michael Evans, I conducted an evaluation of the network which showed that two-thirds of the schools improved at double the rate of the national average. However, as Tom Hatch might have predicted, in a policy environment that was placing pressure on making short-term improvements in test scores and examination results, the network was less successful in achieving long-term transformation.

School-to-school collaborations, networks, and federations proliferated over the first decade or so of this century in England. They were a significant development in building a middle level system of lateral improvement and support. What were the results?

In 2020, UK academics Paul Armstrong, Chris Brown, and Chris Chapman conducted a systematic review of the literature and research on school-to-school collaboration in England. They concluded that "evidence as to how collaboration between schools might directly impact upon student outcomes is limited. Moreover, in the very few studies in which attempts have been made to explore this area the findings are mixed".[19] After two decades of proliferating initiatives resulting from government policy, voluntary efforts, and incentives from quasi-autonomous organizations like the country's National College for School Leadership, the absence of one overall outcome, positive or negative, is not surprising – especially given that the purposes of these networks and funding cycles varied considerably, and still do.

The authors discerned a greater impact on teachers' knowledge of teaching and learning than on student learning outcomes. Moreover, they were able to detect factors that increased or reduced the likelihood of impact. Positive impact was more likely when there was strong and visionary leadership that could also distribute leadership widely, when the purpose of improvement was specific and clear and closely related to teaching and learning, and when considerable attention was paid to developing trust among the participating institutions. All three cases in which I was involved, which looked backwards from the standpoint of proven success, possessed these characteristics in abundance. However, shortage of resources, power imbalances between schools, and increasingly intense environments of inter-school competition, Armstrong and his colleagues argue, threaten all school-to-school collaborations in the end.

In summary, what we can learn from the experience of England is that school-to-school collaborations can successfully improve achievement if the clarity of purpose is lined up with a high trust culture, with strong leadership that also knows when and how to let others take the lead, and with a resource base that does not fizzle out after a year or two. It is also clear that the more competitive a system becomes, the less effective school-to-school collaboration efforts are likely to be. School-to-school collaborations are, in this respect, often initiated as a middle level system to compensate for inter-school competition, but the more competitive a school system becomes with chains of trusts, academies and charter schools, the less successful a middle level system driven by collaborative impulses is likely to be. *Leading From the Middle* will turn into *Leading In the Middle*. Even that will yield limited success. In a highly market-competitive system, *Leading In the Middle* is the silver bullet that shoots itself.

Innovation Networks

While improvement networks are designed to move schools towards better practice and even best practice, innovation networks are about stimulating, seeking out, and spreading next practices that haven't been discovered or even invented yet. Historically, systemically, and numerically, innovation networks have outstripped improvement ones. There are good reasons for this.

Innovation networks generate upbeat engagements with novelty, creativity, and experimentation. They are filled with positive energy and attract volunteers and enthusiasts who are often already outliers in their own schools or districts and so are reaching out to connect with other innovators elsewhere. They like to try something different, experience professional freedom, break a few moulds, move ideas around, network energetically with like-minded thinkers, give extra time and effort to the joy they experience in their work, and find ways to enable their students to feel excited about and connected to their learning. Rather than stimulating educators to innovate for the first time, innovation networks of this sort often attract educators who already have current or prior experiences of innovating.

Many innovation networks are bound and driven by a motivating purpose or shared set of principles. They are often initiated and dignified by the highly regarded ideas of an inspirational and renowned intellectual figurehead such as Ted Sizer and the *Coalition of Essential Schools* or Michael Fullan and the *New Pedagogies for Deep Learning* global network.[20] Schools in these networks come together for periodic conferences and have ongoing or sporadic access to the expertise of the leadership team. The framework of ideas and strategies tends to be more hub-and-spoke or nodal in nature, guided closely by the central team and its subunits, rather than crystalline and self-generating.

The evidence of impact of these branded networks organized around a specific set of principles or bodies of thought is mixed, though. For instance, in line with evaluations conducted by Donna Muncey and Pat McQuillan, Amanda Datnow and her colleagues found that the *Coalition for Essential Schools* network, that was one of five approved and funded models of a Comprehensive School Reform programme by the US Clinton administration, did not outperform matched schools that were not funded under the programme.[21] It was also less effective than models that were more structured and specific in their interventions. Similarly, former US Assistant Secretary of Education, Diane Ravitch, has criticized Comer Schools for pronouncing impressive achievement results without acknowledging that many students unlikely to achieve those results because of behavioural or other problems are pushed out of the schools before the performance measures kick in.

More recently, in 2020, Boston College Professor Karen Arnold, and her co-investigator Georgiana Milhut, published an evaluation of a 25-year-old, for-profit network of innovative schools known as *Big Picture Learning* (BPL). BPL, previously known as the Big Picture Company, was established in the United States, in 1996, by two educators, Dennis Littky and Elliott Washor. It grew out of the US *"small schools"* movement, was influenced by Sizer's Coalition of Essential Schools, and received "significant support from the Bill and Melinda Gates Foundation".[22] The network offers an alternative to traditional high schools and provides learning experiences that are innovative, student-centred, personalized, and surrounded by systems and processes of caring and support. A small size that averages just 120 students per school, close and informal relationships with advisers, individual learning plans, authentic assessments, and supervised internships, are all distinguishing features of BPL.

The network currently comprises 80 schools in the United States and over 250 schools and other places of learning worldwide. It works with numerous partners, and it has received a range of distinguished visitors and supporters, including President Barack Obama. Arnold and Milhut tracked 1900 graduates from six US graduating high school classes and they also interviewed these students' former advisers. The authors then compared the outcomes of BPL with published outcomes data from a prominent and starkly contrasting school network known as the Knowledge is Power Program (KIPP) of over 250 US schools that also push for educational equity. KIPP schools are part of a No Excuses movement that adopts very different methodologies to BPL. These emphasize hard work, extra time, parental contracts, prescribed teaching methods, and authoritarian approaches to classroom control. How do BPL schools stack up against their educational opposite?

Evaluating BPL in relation to its own goals of "adult self-fulfillment, meaningful work, financial security and upward mobility, healthy relationships, and civic engagement", Arnold and Milhut conclude that there is a "high degree of success in facilitating student engagement, social capital, personal and vocational development, and high school completion among low-income, urban students".[23] Two out of the Gates Foundation's three R's it established for small high schools – relevance and relationships – exhibited success, the evaluation notes. The outcomes are strong, the authors say, on "student development in personal, interpersonal, and vocational development".[24] However, they also caution that the numbers are so small and the relationships so intense that improvement may have been a result of what is known as the Hawthorne or halo effect – the sheer fact that students are getting unusual amounts of attention – rather than due to specific design features of the network. With 80 US schools and an average of 120 students per school, it's also important to ask whether this level of investment for a grand national total of students that is no more than four good-sized traditional high schools, would be sustainable on a larger scale.

By contrast, measures of "college academic readiness and degree attainment", along with performance in science and mathematics – the third R of rigour in Gates's original triumvirate – are mixed. While students do well in getting to college, "they graduate at lower rates than the overall U.S. average and at somewhat lower rates than published results from the KIPP No Excuses model school network".[25]

Voluntary and foundation supported networks, it seems, have an uneven impact, and they find it difficult to get their networks to leave a broader footprint within public systems. In this sense, instead of becoming another way to lead whole systems from the middle, these sorts of innovation networks turn into outliers of the existing system, or even safety valves for rebellious teachers and students that leave the rest of the system intact.

Perhaps there is a case, then, for reconsidering a role for government involvement at the top, so networks can become a significant part of a dynamic middle. Yet, government-run networks can quickly become just another tool to implement policies bureaucratically. There is, however, another way for governments to get involved in network development and operation. That is to work with partners, third parties, or semi-independent agencies to develop networks that are connected to policy but not oppressed by top-down bureaucracies.

One example was the *Alberta Initiative for School Improvement (AISI)*. This network which, despite its name, was more about innovation than improvement, was established through collaboration between the Alberta Teachers' Association and the Alberta government's education department to promote teacher-driven innovation across the province. The initiative, which ran for almost 15 years, involved teams of teachers in 95 per cent of the province's schools. It required all projects to be collaboratively designed, to be reported and reflected on by educators, and to be shared with other schools at an annual meeting and online.

In 2009, I was asked to lead a team of expert researchers from the United States, Canada, and Finland, to evaluate the impact of AISI.[26] Although multiple statistical strategies were used to try and separate out the relative impact of AISI on student achievement compared to other policies and initiatives, the range of self-designed innovations was so broad and varied across the province's schools that it proved impossible to disentangle the specific effects of AISI from all other policy influences. However, the overall performance of Alberta during AISI's operation was strong – scoring as one of the highest systems in the world on the OECD's international PISA results in student performance and on the OECD's related measures of strong teachers' work cultures. Consistent with the OECD's second set of findings were findings from our evaluation pointing to measurable positive impact of AISI and its opportunities for innovation on teacher satisfaction and motivation.

A second example of innovation networks that have government involvement at state or national levels is the *Northwest Rural Innovation and Student Engagement* (NW RISE) network. Comprising more than 30 remote rural US schools, this network was supported with federal government funding, supplemented by modest state and local government and foundation investments over time, to improve student achievement in rural and remote communities. My Boston College colleague, Dennis Shirley, and I, along with our lead researcher, Michael O'Connor, supported the Oregon-based network from 2012 to 2019.[27]

Led by Danette Parsley, the NW RISE network aimed to raise achievement by developing students' engagement with their learning, their communities, and their lives, and it involved state education representatives and leaders from schools and districts in five participating states. The schools met in two face-to-face meetings per year, and online in between, to plan and then reflect on curriculum and other improvements in "job-alike" groups of subject-based, grade-based, or role-based educators. In a 2017 survey, over 93 per cent of participating educators reported that the network had resulted in improvements in teacher and student engagement and student learning.[28] Some of the public testimonies made by once embittered and disillusioned veteran teachers about the network's impact on transforming their own practice and professional motivation had an almost revelatory and confessional quality about them.

Parsley and her team worked with state education agency staff and other partners to foster and support a grassroots network, rather than imposing a network in a top-down way. This was what led the NW RISE team to turn to Dennis Shirley and me as collaborators to co-develop and test out a set of design principles with the team that would help educators to create their own network based on their own needs and purposes.

AISI and NW RISE demonstrate that innovation networks can create widespread and sustained changes in teachers' awareness, understandings, practices, and collaborative relationships, in ways that positively affect student engagement with learning. At their best, because they work in partnership with policy, but are also somewhat independent of it, their chances of impact, spread and sustainability are greater than in voluntary or commercially based networks. They can become important and impressive forms of *Leadership From the Middle*.

There is a caveat, though. Networks that are connected to but not driven by government have greater promise than almost any others in education. Yet nothing lasts forever. As cynics sometimes say, there are few or no permanent friends in politics. Governments change. Leaders turn over. New agendas emerge. Old ones are abandoned. AISI lasted for over a decade under a relatively stable political regime that cut across conservative and then socialist governments. During the long years of Tony Blair's Labour government in the UK, semi-autonomous government agencies sprang up like the National College for School Leadership, and the Specialist Schools and Academies Trust, and all kinds of networks supporting innovation and teacher professional development flourished as a result – even if the results were mixed. But in Alberta and England alike, the rise of populist versions of conservatism saw all these innovation networks terminated, or have their funding withdrawn.

Networks connected with governments that don't become implementation arms for them can have considerable impact – directly on teacher learning and teacher quality, and indirectly on student learning – when packaged with compatible policy measures focused on equity, improvement, well-being, and so on. They can become a powerful mechanism for *Leadership From the Middle* and for moving towards what British scholars have called a self-improving school system. Eventually, though, when governments collapse, the networks often fold with them. Voluntary or commercial networks are more able to ride the waves of political change, but they do not have the strength or connectedness to policy to be an effective system for *Leadership From the Middle*. Indeed, often, in a system of free market competition, multiple networks can undermine the very coherence and cohesion that *Leadership From the Middle* requires.

Six Principles of Network Design

We now have a formidable knowledge base on the nature, types, and relative impact of different kinds of networks, within education and beyond. I have also drawn on my own experience of helping to design and evaluate school networks internationally. Many educators, especially the most passionate and innovative ones, love networks because it is here that they can share and learn about new ideas, meet like-minded colleagues, and experience joy in their professional work. But when we get a chance to start a network, to join one, or to use it to help to *Lead From the Middle*, it's not enough just to be enthusiastic and upbeat about networks and networking, and to think they will be awesome and amazing by their very nature.

Networks can have different kinds of structures and cultures. These need to be designed deliberately, in an evidence-informed way. Pursuing the promise of networks must not blind us to their many pitfalls. Networks can be superficial, waste people's time, exploit teachers' goodwill, joyfully implement bad ideas, exclude outsiders, and turn into self-validating cults. They can suffer from both under- and over-participation, groupthink, vagueness of focus, slowness of pace in moving to action, lack of visible products or short-term benefits, and excessive efforts to secure top-down regulation of the network in its purpose, processes, and outcomes.[29]

These are just a few of the threats and risks that demand professional honesty, realism, and shrewdness among those who have been charged with the responsibility for creating a network, or who have been given the opportunity to join one. Drawing on the arguments and evidence of this chapter, therefore, let's look at six key design

---

SIX NETWORK PRINCIPLES

- Shared Vision, Goals & Focus – what do you want to accomplish?

- Collaborative Activities – what will you do?

- Membership & Citizenship – who's in & what do they expect?

- Leadership – how do you steer and support?

- Knowledge Circulation – how will you share & use what is learned?

- Sustainability – how will it survive, thrive & eventually expire?

Figure 6.2 Six Principles of Network Design

considerations, as illustrated in Figure 6.2, that Danette Parsley and I have identified for creating and sustaining an effective network that can lead a system from the middle. The chapter will then close with a description of a network my colleagues and I at the University of Ottawa have created and are leading based on those design principles.

1. Shared Vision, Goals, and Focus

What is the network about? What purpose underpin it? Networks can't just be about sharing practices or any other activity for their own sake. So, what is the point of a network? Who will it benefit? And how? These questions need to be addressed in the beginning stages of network design so that members can be clear about what they hope to gain from participation, and what impact they might have as a result. This helps to establish a network's identity, develop shared ownership among participants, and create a positive network culture. Is the network designed to benefit teachers, parents, or students, for example? Is it about improvement or innovation, or implementation of a government priority – or some combination of these things? Will it seek to raise standards, improve equity, enhance well-being, or stimulate professional learning and motivation, for instance? Will it focus on assessment for learning, improvement of literacy, or attending to students' mental health? Or will it improve learning and well-being for certain groups of students such as those with learning disabilities, or ones who are living in poverty? Some of the most effective networks are guided by high-priority local needs that are connected to, but not merely targets for, implementing existing initiatives and priorities.

Mark Hadfield and Chris Chapman have suggested that network members should "engage critically and honestly with colleagues about what they want to achieve and the values on which this decision is based". It's important to be open about issues and problems, they continue, "as there is no point in setting unrealistic and unachievable aims".[30]

There are no shortcuts for establishing a genuinely shared vision and goals for a network. Achieving clarity and reaching consensus requires substantial time, careful facilitation, and a core group of motivated and invested participants with a high tolerance for ambiguity. An effective network that leads from the middle must belong to the participants.

It cannot be borrowed or rented from a corporate-style branded model that exists elsewhere and it cannot be imposed simply to implement government priorities.

2. Collaborative Activities

A big concern for potential members of a network is what they will do when they join it. Networks motivate people to stick with them when those people can look forward to engaging in a core practice or activity whenever members of the network meet. In NW RISE, educators placed high value on creating innovative curricula together that would engage their students more effectively. In Alberta and Ontario, designing and sharing innovations were the central practices. Network members might coach and be critical friends for each other on how to tackle difficult problems in their work. They might share their own writing if they are in a national writing project. They might develop alternative forms of assessment.[31] These are just some of the examples of what educational networks can do and have done. Whatever the activity that network members value and undertake, it's important to avoid becoming a "meeting" culture of clusters or nodes that are dedicated to implementing externally prescribed changes.

3. Membership and Citizenship

One of the first and most obvious issues when starting a network is deciding who's in and who's out. Sometimes, networks recruit enthusiastic innovators or volunteer subscribers to a new programme, pedagogy, or improvement strategy. Conversely, schools may be "invited" to join a network so that they'll learn how to improve or be more likely to implement a policy initiative. There is often a paradox of network participation. The schools most inclined to join may be the least likely to benefit. Volunteers who are quick off the mark in joining new networks may already have benefited from belonging to others before. Conversely, schools that are more reticent may need network connections and supports the most.

Volunteers are dream participants for network designers. But they are not immune to problems and threats. While they can be eager to get engaged, they are also prone to burnout because of over-participation. Volunteers at the front edge of change can also suffer from the fate of all innovative groups that educational change expert Seymour Sarason famously described in the 1970s – a tendency to ascribe actual or attributed feelings of arrogance and superiority to members associated with innovations.[32] If recruitment is badly managed, pushback from outside the network will soon seal its fate.

Completely open calls for network participation are therefore inadvisable. Some sort of guidance in recruitment by network designers can help achieve a better overall balance. Designers can actively invite schools who are not normally in the first waves of change because they are geographically isolated from governments or universities, or because they are sceptical about transient change agendas. Invitational recruitment of this kind is highly dependent on personal communication and trusting relationships between school participants on the one hand and network designers in universities, teacher unions, or governments, for example, on the other.

Once networks have been established, a clear strategy is needed to manage relations with schools outside the network, and with schools whose applications were rejected too. This is a second problem that Sarason identified as accompanying all innovative efforts – the challenge of managing "foreign relations" with jealous peers, and suspicious rivals.[33] Network members and leaders must be vigilant about demonstrating recognition and respect for other innovations and innovators; about actively listening to people in bureaucracies, finance departments, legal departments and the like who have less of a network mentality; and about being mindful and empathetic towards rather than resentful about how the network and its members might be perceived from the outside.

4. Leadership

Unless they have a hub-and-spoke structure, networks are not all or only about chaotic energy, distributed responsibility, lateral interaction, and unpredictable change. Networks attract progressives and romantics who are drawn to relationships rather than bureaucracy as instigators of change. They appeal to socialists and democrats who welcome flat structures and decision-making processes that are equitable and inclusive, rather than top-down and privileged. And they can also be a source of fascination for libertarians and anarchists who resist and resent any forms of oppression and control.

But networks are not headless entities. The internet is the apogee of all networks. But even and perhaps especially there, the private data of people all over the planet ultimately rests in the hands of organizations controlled by some of the richest and most powerful men in the world. In professional and cultural networks, it is sometimes individual charismatic leaders, including thought leaders, who insist that their cult-like followings interact laterally with one another but vertically with them. They remain the patriarchs or matriarchs of the entire group and its direction, watching over every interaction within the network that they ultimately regulate and monitor.

Even if networks are not tightly controlled at the top by surveillance or dependency, they can still operate in ways that can lead to exclusion as well as inclusion, and to tacit forms of leadership that advance some interests over others. In networks and in life, people tend to gravitate towards others like themselves. They may be communities of enthusiastic extroverts who, like the 1980s band Depeche Mode, "just can't get enough" of anything.[34] They may be generational groups like baby boomers or millennials who share similar interests and experience the world in similar ways. They may be women caucusing with women, men with men, and people of the same feather who predictably flock together.

It's an understandable and desirable feature of networks that people gather around common interests and identities, like teachers of the same subject, or educators who work in small rural schools, for example. In the US NW RISE network, for example, when participants were asked what they valued most from the in-person convenings, they highlighted "talking with other colleagues about issues we share", "meeting other grade-level teachers that have the same concerns I have", and "talking to people who do what I do".

But it's also the job of a network leader to ensure that subgroup commonality doesn't degenerate into group-think; that teachers in the suburbs don't fail to connect with and learn from colleagues in indigenous communities or in schools coping with child poverty (and vice versa), for example. Diversity and inclusion of expertise, perspectives and identities are a constant obligation for network leadership.

By design or by default, by accident or by subterfuge, networks always have leaders. Leaderless networks are oxymorons. The development of effective networks depends on high-quality network leadership at the head of it all that initiates, supports, and steers the networks over time. This leadership should inspire engagement, provide clarity of purpose, and maintain discipline in adhering to protocols, and rules of participation. Network leaders should demonstrate public support and provide inspiration through words and actions. They should help bring innovative ideas and expertise into the network to shake up assumptions, disrupt complacency, identify threats, and seek out opportunities. They should pay attention to evidence and research, monitor impacts and outcomes, and watch out for the network getting overly exuberant about networking for its own sake.

Network leadership and design is also about promoting a culture of collaborative learning that stretches out distributed leadership across the network so that ideas can emerge quickly and get circulated efficiently. Network activities should maximize real collaboration time, which leads to high levels of participant energy and engagement. However, too much self-direction in the beginning stages can also be frustrating for participants. Network organizers can play an important role in providing just enough scaffolded support without being too constrictive or prescriptive and with an eye towards gradual release of responsibility among network members themselves.

All leaders within a network should be able and know how and when to pull people into networking for change whenever they can by encouraging, inspiring, and enlightening existing and potential network members. Leaders should also push people with the right combination of pressure and support into and through zones of discomfort when it is necessary. When does a core idea need challenging and deepening – whether it's collaborative inquiry, growth mindsets, engagement, playful learning, or something else? Are all network members pulling their weight? Do some members lack network capital – the knowledge and skills of how to network – and can leaders guide them into how to get more out of their participation?

Hugh Busher and Keith Hodgkinson suggest that several leadership activities and principles are conducive to closer collaboration within a network.[35] These include:

- rotating chairpersons and venues for meetings;
- ensuring that all participants take responsibility for engagement;
- building good relationships with the wider system (Sarason's foreign relations);
- acknowledging potential areas of disagreement and managing valuable debate;
- devolving as much responsibility as possible to those closest to practice.

The skills and capacities of network leadership can be learned. In the RATL network that Dennis Shirley and I evaluated, we learned that leaders who had been historically isolated in rural schools didn't already possess great skill in networking. Our co-researchers –Michael Evans and Corrie Stone-Johnson – found that "networking can be learned and that the presence of a support system for network leaders may enhance the effectiveness and quality of participation for both individual schools and the network at large".[36]

What is it important for network leaders to do, then? Steer and disturb; do not direct or disown. Appoint a representative group of network members to lead activities and make decisions. This increases ownership and ensures the network is relevant and useful to everyone A third-party entity can act as a backbone for the network and its leaders and manage tasks such as facilitation and logistics. Partners, such as university researchers, can provide both appreciative and critical feedback to support the network and help it achieve its goals. Outside ideas, multiple exemplars, evidence-informed practices, and exchanges with other networks can all maintain healthy disturbance and prevent the network from becoming routine and stale. Specific insights and examples from research and practice within and outside the network can provoke and support improvement and change. In these respects, network leaders can steer the network without micromanaging it and disturb the network without dissipating its efforts.

5. Knowledge Circulation

Knowledge circulation is about how knowledge moves around so that many people can benefit from it. Knowledge circulation moves beyond more traditional ideas about knowledge utilization which suggest that someone has the knowledge, and that other people use it. It also gets beyond knowledge mobilization which implies, in almost military terms, that knowledge is something like an army that gets mobilized by intellectual generals away from the frontline, for other people's benefit. Knowledge circulation is more about designing systems and processes that move knowledge around efficiently and effectively, wherever it originates from.

Networks thrive when new knowledge, tools, ideas, and strategies are circulated throughout the network and beyond, stretching out to the whole school system and other systems. Knowledge circulation is not a process of one-way dissemination. It is about network participants engaging in crystalline and not just hub-and-spoke activities with each other that they initiate themselves within empowering structures developed by the design team. It's also important that participants engage in parallel learning and development activities within and beyond their own schools outside the network, so they don't get smothered by their own networks at the cost of other professional engagements.

Working with schools outside an immediate network to circulate knowledge among all of them is an essential part of spreading out what the network is learning and achieving. This needs to be done from a standpoint of humility in which network schools are not just teachers but also learners. Network schools must avoid seeming like know-it-alls who tell everyone else what's good for them. These issues of how to manage network relations raise important questions of leadership and sustainability.

6. Resources and Sustainability

Networks require resources. It's unlikely they will even get off the ground if their existence depends entirely on overtaxed teachers and leaders dedicating more and more of their time and energy to managing day-to-day operations of the network. Leaders can and should procure and provide resources that create release time for participants to engage in face-to-face as well as online network activity, ensure that educators are not overwhelmed by a profusion and confusion of networks to which they are meant to belong, and connect the networks and their members to other relevant organizations and communities.

Not too long after a network gets started, and once it is up and running and people can see the value of it, it must then start to address, in a good way, how and when it might end, and what its legacy might be. Sustainability, however, is usually one of the last things an organization or network thinks about. It's usually quite late on when people start to worry and wonder what will happen when the funding stops, the grant runs out, and the focus shifts to something else. Will it all continue? Where will the money come from next? Will everyone discover that they've committed themselves for nothing?

There are four things to consider about sustainability:

- Nothing lasts forever, and most networks last for a lot less time than that.
- The time to think about sustainability is near the start of a network, not the end.
- The longevity of a network depends on how it manages leadership succession.
- Sustainability is not just a matter of time or making something last.

First, *there are no forever networks*. So, does that make them a bad investment? A common question I get asked when I am recording podcasts is what I want my legacy to be. It's a mistake, I say, to try and plan your legacy. The moment you do, everything becomes all about you. When I was a child in primary school, my best teacher, Mary Hindle, did not know what her legacy would be when she taught me. She inspired me to become an educator like her, though, by the engaging nature of her pedagogy and by the way she understood me, even though I wasn't always the easiest child to teach. Her influence on me became my influence on others – teachers, schools and even governments all over the world. That's a legacy she could never have imagined. Her practices, ethics, and care towards me were what defined her legacy. The skills we practice, memories we create, and relationships we build with others that stick with them – these things are our legacies.

Educational networks eventually end, like everything else. What matters is that the good things they represent persist in new practices, better relationships, and broadening influence, in ways that help teachers and students in many places and over many years to improve what they do in the years to come.

Second, sustainability should never be an afterthought of network development; the last truck-stop on a highway of eventual disappointment and regret. Near the very beginning of a network's development, everyone needs to be involved in addressing the question of how it will continue when start-up funding disappears. Involve participants early in this question. If they see the network is benefiting them, they will assume collective responsibility for finding further time and resources in the future. The answer to the sustainability question is not for the network's founders to shake some magic money tree for more resources but for everyone to treat sustainability as a shared responsibility.

Even so, networks, like other initiatives, can collapse at any time. Funders may hit a financial crisis. Economic collapses put pressure on all granting bodies, including governments. Policy climates may shift from supporting innovation and creativity to going back to basics. Leaders may change, and with them, the projects that they favour. For these reasons, it's essential that while everyone in a network should plan for the long term, they should also live each day as if it is their last. People in networks should bank capital for the future; not financial capital, but professional capital of new knowledge, new skills and expertise, and new relationships and partnerships that will endure long after the network has dissolved. A question everyone in a network should ask themselves from time to time is "What is one thing that I can learn or do differently right now in this network, that will last a lifetime?" Sustainability needs to be a perennial mindset, not an appended afterthought.

Third: *sustainable success depends on effective leadership succession.* Leadership succession is the stuff of history, myth, and drama. Only in death did Queen Elizabeth II of England give way to her septuagenarian son. In the award-winning drama series, *Succession*, the family patriarch, Logan Roy, taunts and toys with his own adult children as they seek to seize his reins of power.[37] Yet even they fared better than the son of the Greek God Kronos. He was eaten by his own father so he could never take his father's place. The hardest part of leadership is learning to let go.

Charismatic leaders can attract adoring followers in a network. But when these leaders leave, those followers can soon become lost. The answer to the common challenge of network leadership succession is to treat it as an issue for the whole group, not just for how one leader can or should follow another. Succession is not just about how networks persist over time, from one leader to the next. It is about creating a robust organization with many kinds of leaders who hold it all together so that leadership and success do not become overly dependent on any one of them, and so that leadership at the top emerges from a deep pool of rising talent in the whole network.

Fourth: *sustainability is about thinking and planning for how it will all end.* This raises a provocative thought: planned obsolescence. If they are successful, networks will eventually start to supplant, rather than merely supplement, traditional hierarchical and bureaucratic decision-making structures. As a network develops and matures, people who have the most ties with other network members gain easy access to information and knowledge. They discover they can communicate with many other educators, including traditional system leaders. As a result, they become increasingly prominent compared to peripheral or isolated members. They may move to the core of the middle, or towards the top, or out of the network altogether.

In this sense, a network's sustainability is not ultimately about its own longevity, but about how embedded its work, relationships, and multiple ways of *Leading From the Middle* have become within the wider system. A network may come to an end not because it fades or fails, but because its success leads to it becoming obsolete as a separate entity. Planned obsolescence is a bold and by no means bad goal for a network to have.

Leading From the Middle in Action: The Canadian Playful Schools Network

What might a network look like that incorporates all these design principles, that achieves the maximum possible benefits, and that also boldly and bluntly confronts the ubiquitous risks. At the start of 2022, my University of Ottawa colleagues and I had an opportunity to address this question by designing a Canada-wide network of more than 40 schools practising and seeking to deepen play-based learning for marginalized and underserved populations. With a grant of C$2.7 million from the LEGO Foundation, spread across 18 months, what design decisions has our team made based on our research and experience base of network development?

The Canadian Playful School Network (CPSN) sprouted from a discussion with representatives of the LEGO Foundation in their Learning Through Play programme.[38] A joint direction emerged from two different but compatible interests within our university team and at the LEGO Foundation respectively:

1 Researching the relative strengths and weaknesses of different modes of learning that had become prominent by necessity during the COVID-19 pandemic: especially learning outdoors (*green* learning) and learning digitally (*screen*-based learning).
2 Building a Canadian network of schools supporting play-based learning as part of a wider global network, with a focus on supporting marginalized and vulnerable students after the COVID-19 pandemic.

My co-investigator, Dr Trista Hollweck, a former teacher, school district consultant, and school administrator, with province-wide experience of organizing professional networks, prepared a proposal with me to the LEGO Foundation following several months of discussion with its staff. This proposal also resulted from collaboration with six other faculty members who I introduced in the Preface.

The *purpose* of the network is to develop student engagement and well-being, as two of the keys to student success and fulfilment, by learning though play.[39] The targeted populations are marginalized students who have traditionally been underserved by Canadian school systems. They include indigenous students, students in poor rural communities, newcomer immigrants and refugees, historically black Canadians, minority French cultures, and students with special needs. The network focuses on the middle years of grades 5–8 where pressures of top-down accountability, content-based curricula, and physically larger early-adolescents make play-based approaches harder for schools to establish. One intent of the network is to work with schools to learn how they experience and overcome these barriers in their efforts to use play based pedagogies.

The CPSN network is not meant to idealize, romanticize, or uncritically celebrate the value of play. It pushes educators into thinking harder about different kinds of play, into considering when forms of play can be harmful as well as helpful, or superficial rather than deep, and into developing empathy for and ways of engaging with educators, families, and community members who may be critical about the use of too much play in schools.

Four modes of play, separately, or in combination, are the focal points of schools' efforts in playful learning.

1   *Green* play – including outdoor learning, gardening and tree planting, indigenous learning on the land, environmental education, and education for sustainability.
2   *Screen* play – including simulation, gaming, virtual interaction, coding, video animation, and the use of drone technologies.
3   *Machine or makerspace play* – including robotics, mechanical and electrical construction, 3D printing, and everyday materials such as paper, wood, and glue.
4   *Everything in between* – especially the use of language in play through literature, music, slam poetry, and group conversation, for example.

Using clear criteria about the modes of play, the grade levels involved, and the populations being served, a call was sent out on social media and through the Ottawa team's own networks, for school teams including 2–4 educators and a school administrator to apply. Applications were reviewed by at least two Ottawa faculty members with a view to having a final grouping of around six schools in each of seven provinces.

Canada is constitutionally unique in being an officially bilingual and multicultural society. It consists of ten provinces and two territories which administer the nation's K-12 schools autonomously. The project is, in almost every respect, bilingual in internal and external communications and in a school sample that comprises about one-third that are French language and culture in nature, and two-thirds that are English. The focus on marginalized populations recognizes Canada's multicultural and inclusive nature. The University of Ottawa, situated in the nation's capital, is on the unceded territory of the Algonquin people and is Canada's only fully bilingual university. It is a public university, and the location of this project and network headquarters there not only lends the network legitimacy, but also gives it a mark of independence, accountability, and integrity because the organizing body serves no private, commercial, or political interests.

In terms of *Leadership From the Middle*, the network is connected to provincial policy leaders in five out of the seven provinces where pre-existing relationships and trust with CPSN faculty members were already established. The connection with policy is not so that the network will implement policies and priorities. It is so that broader provincial policy systems will learn from the activities and developments of its own network schools and potentially reach around 1.3 million students in the targeted grade range in wider provincial systems. The network is not an arm of policy or an alternative to it. It is a separate entity from which policy leaders can learn in a deliberately designed way.

The CPSN network started up in hub-and-spoke mode. Each school team was virtually onboarded and coached for 90 minutes before network activities commenced to collect updated information about their work and focus, aspirations for the future, and perceptions of obstacles, along with ideas about how they might overcome them. The onboarding has also given the Ottawa team an opportunity to connect with every school team and to explain the network's purpose, structure, and design.

The onboarding meetings were followed by a virtual launch for all the teams to engage in together so there was opportunity to see each other and to meet the whole project team for the first time, as well as engage in some initial orientation activities. During and after the virtual launch, school teams were placed in virtual playgroups or nodes of around six schools per playgroup. The groups were chosen, defined, and facilitated by research faculty and project staff. The groupings were based on evidence of the school teams' interests and areas of focus in their applications and onboarding meetings, and on faculty research interests that form a basis for the expertise they can best offer, and for a future research and publishing agenda that will arise from the project. Playgroups were organized among English schools and French schools respectively around themes like special needs, land-based learning, middle years emphases, and so forth. The playgroups meet twice, virtually, over a six-month period. The job of facilitators of these groups is not just to enable school teams to share and celebrate their practice, but also to deepen and challenge it through interactions with each other and with various experts and thought leaders inside and outside the university faculty.

If the playgroups are somewhat pre-structured – something that the network literature advises in the early stages of network development – a second form of networking is more free-flowing in nature. Here, school teams are established to set playdates around interests and top-ics that they define. They are invited to create their own adventures. There will also be webinars run by members of the faculty, associated thought leaders and partners, and people in the schools themselves. The purpose of the playdates is to try and move the network from the nodal structure of the set playgroups that are facilitated by different faculty members, to a more crystalline structure, where school teams engage autonomously with each other. The project's network design is represented in Figure 6.3.

An international advisory board of 13 distinguished and diverse international experts representing the four modes of play, different marginalized communities, and expertise in innovation and network development gives feedback to the team. It engages with playgroups and playdates at their request. It contributes to webinars and a culmi-nating conference. It also disturbs the network and gives it things to think about, with new ideas and critical feedback.[40]

Research on the network and its development is a vital part of the project so that, unlike many other networks, it does not remain

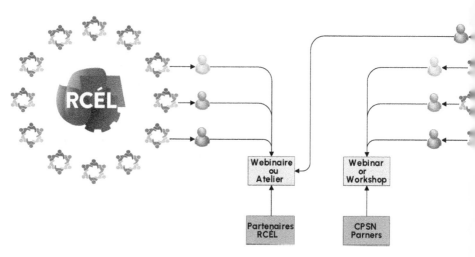

Figure 6.3 The CPSN Network Structure (created by the CPSN design team)

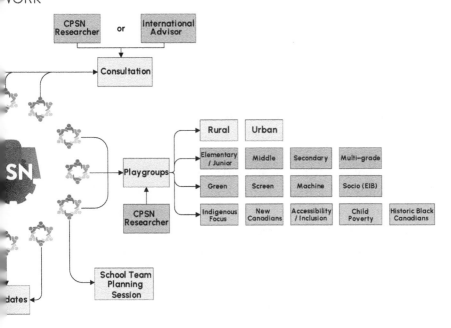

immune from objective evaluation about its development and its impact. Six strands of research among our faculty team comprise:

1 *Scoping literature reviews* on areas like green learning, special educational needs, and educational network development.
2 *Action research* on the work carried out in virtual playgroups and playdates.
3 *In-person visits* to and data collection from a sample of the network's schools.
4 *Social network analysis* to determine how network interactions develop and change over time, and with what effect.
5 *Baseline data* against which future network development beyond this opening phase of the project can be compared.
6 *Exit data* on educators' self-reports on the network's impact on them and their students.

Resources are allocated to each school team to cover up to seven days of teacher release time per school, to reimburse expenses for travel, accommodation, and replacement teacher costs for a culminating conference, and to provide up to C$5,000 per team for other expenses involving costs for technology, materials, and procuring specialized expertise.

Sustainability is uncertain, as this book goes to press, as the funding environment at a time of global economic insecurity and rapid organizational turnover is unpredictable, and leadership and priorities change in foundations just like they do everywhere else. So, from the outset, everyone on the project team is gathering evidence and experience that will have long-term benefit beyond the project, and similar conversations are being held with school teams. In essence, we will seek to live the paradoxical motto of planning for the long term and living each day as if it was our last!

The CPSN is an ambitious project where we are trying to design an effective and impactful network in an evidence-based way that will benefit students' engagement, and well-being, and use an increasingly sophisticated system of *Leadership From the Middle* to spread ideas and insights beyond the network to schools across the country. In summary, to return the six network design principles described earlier:

1 The network has *clear purposes, goals, and focal points* of play-based learning for engagement and well-being, with underserved populations in grades where play-based approaches encounter many obstacles.

2 The *activities* of playgroups and playdates define the core of the network's work.

3 In terms of *membership and citizenship*, there have been clear rules and transparent processes of *recruitment and participation*. The network is embedded in and connected to the work of traditional policy systems without being controlled or regulated by them.

4 *Network leadership* commenced with a hub-and-spoke structure as is advisable in the early stages of network development. It is moving through nodal to more crystallized forms of *Leadership From the Middle*. There are clear provisions of *resource support*, especially for educators' time to collaborate and network together. The CPSN network is housed in a *public and accountable* university with transparent and ethical processes of financing, development and research, objective databases, and absences of political self-interest or commercial profitability.

5 *Network knowledge will circulate* with increasing complexity through playgroups and playdates. The network is also being purposely *disturbed* by the advisory board and other partners so that its knowledge base keeps on moving and changing.

6 Planning for *sustainability* includes the possible end of the network in its present form, being mindful of the learnings being gathered that might last beyond the network, and considering the prospects of planned obsolescence, when the success of the network may no longer require its continuation.

Conclusion

Leadership From the Middle through networks takes schools beyond their districts and even their states and provinces as they forge ways to lead together for positive change that increase inclusion and advance equity in a post-pandemic world. Networks can be add-ons to existing systems. They can also provide alternatives to mainstream systems.

At some point, though, all forms of *Leadership From the Middle* rub up against existing systems and raise questions about those systems themselves. How do systems need to change to fully embrace *Leadership From the Middle* not as a temporary intervention or innovation, but as a permanent form of educational life? This is the subject of the final chapter.

7

LEADING SYSTEMS FROM THE MIDDLE

Leadership From the Middle is not self-justifying. It's not a new policy or strategy that should exist for its own sake. *Leadership From the Middle*, rather, may be the best approach we currently have to move towards a better and more effective system that provides smooth and continuous support for everyone. What does *Leadership From the Middle* look like when it becomes part of a whole system that moves forward to achieve excellence, equity, and inclusion for all students? What does and should a system look like when *Leadership From the Middle* is an integral part of it? This chapter examines three alternatives: trust-based systems, self-improving school systems, and social movements.

Trust-based Systems

One of the things that holds systems together and gives them coherence and direction is the existence of high levels of trust. Nations, like schools and school systems, differ greatly in their levels of trust. You can tell this when you cross international borders. For more than 30 years, I have lived on one side or the other of the Canadian–US border and travelled across it regularly. Although my wife and I made some of the best friends we ever had during the 15 years we were resident in the United States, one of the most challenging aspects of America is the simple act of getting in and out.

In 2018, we returned to Canada to be close to three of our grandchildren. On one of the next occasions when I moved back over the border to give a speech, the immigration officer looked at my file and scanned his computer.

"Do you still have a Green Card?" he asked, gruffly.
"No. I handed it in a year ago to this day at the border", I said.
I passed him a piece of paper.
"Here's my Certificate of Abandonment", I said.

It's a strange term to adopt for deciding to move from a country and renounce employment and permanent residence rights. Abandonment suggests lack of responsibility or commitment; something a bit shameful, even callous, or uncaring. In law, abandonment means "to cast away, leave or desert, as property or a child". So, leaving a country where you've lived and made a constructive contribution to the economy and society for 15 years is construed as abandoning the country as if it were an unwanted child.

The language of leaving the United States is no less delicate than the language of arriving. Come to the United States to be a resident, and if you are not yet, or not at all, a full citizen, you will see your identity staring back at you from the page, as that of an "Alien". Like some unwanted intruder from outer space, to gain entry you must answer a battery of questions including "Have you ever participated in genocide?" I wonder if anyone has ever answered "Yes" to this question, or perhaps confessed, "Just a bit, but that was a long time ago now". Everyone's answer is going to be "No" (unless they can't read the form, of course), but they must still write it down and say it anyway. Otherwise, unless it is there in black and white, off they might go, liquidating an entire race of human beings before you know it.

The immigration officer turned back to me. "Why did you leave?" he growled.
"Grandchildren", I replied. "Three of them." "They all live in Ottawa."
"Well, I guess that's a good reason", he conceded, and sent me on my way.

Entering or leaving the United States is a process that is shot through with low trust. You are under suspicion from the start. You are not welcomed or embraced for coming to join the land of the free and the home of the brave, to embrace life, liberty, and the pursuit of happiness. Instead, you are presumed to be up to no good until proven otherwise. Everyone, practically, is an object of suspicion. This especially applies at security.

Of course, with good cause, in an age of global terrorism, there is every reason to have airport security, metal detectors, body scans, and the like. It's not the technology of security that distinguishes one nation or system from another, though, but how security officers behave. In most countries, they are professional, polite, systematic, and discreet. If you make a mistake, like leaving a Swiss army knife in your bag (which I did once), it's assumed to be an oversight; one that any reasonable person could make. In the United States, though, you can hear security officers from the other side of the room, even before you turn the corner to line up. Like sergeants conducting a drill for a platoon of marine recruits, they are barking out orders to everyone within earshot. "Liquids *must* be in a ziplock bag." "*Take out* cellphones, laptops and all electronic devices." "*Remove* your shoes and belts." Suddenly, you are not a passenger, a citizen, a customer, or even a human being with basic dignity. You are a subordinate, like an adolescent in junior high school, who is clearly intransigent or incompetent and needs to have every instruction shouted out at top volume to assure your compliance. This is a system of low trust, or even no-trust, top-down leadership that says a lot about the low levels of trust in the entire society.

Compared to other developed economies, the United States suffers from two closely connected extremes. It has one of the highest levels of economic inequality. It also has some of the lowest levels of trust of all developed economies and democracies. In their best-selling books, *The Spirit Level* and the *Inner Level*, epidemiologists Richard Wilkinson and Kate Pickett show that high levels of economic inequality are associated with a vast range of negative social outcomes.[1] In places like the United States and United Kingdom, growing economic inequality manifests itself in high rates of drug use and alcoholism, disturbing levels of depression and anxiety, health-threatening levels of eating disorders, distressing incidences of bullying in school and violent crime in the community – and low levels of trust. The Nordic countries and the Netherlands are diametric opposites of these trends.

Some years ago, I wrote a journal article called "Teaching and Betrayal" based on interviews with 50 teachers about their emotional experiences of their work.² Trust, I argued, takes months or years to build. Betrayal can happen in an instant. Many betrayals are not deliberate acts of cruelty or manipulation but thoughtless acts of neglect due to concentrating on other priorities or becoming overwhelmed. A big part of building trust is avoiding betrayal. There were, I showed, three kinds of betrayal:

- *Competence betrayal*: when colleagues or administrators thought that teachers couldn't do their jobs properly and weren't competent or qualified.
- *Contract betrayal*: when colleagues thought that teachers didn't follow through on what they had agreed to do, or they didn't pull their weight and try hard enough.
- *Communication betrayal*: when educators said the wrong thing, failed to offer praise or positive feedback, or didn't connect with their fellow professionals.

The key insight is that most incidents of what administrators and teachers' colleagues believed to be contract or competence betrayal (not putting in enough effort or not doing things properly) were really the result of communication betrayal – making judgements about people without really understanding their actions, motivations, or other issues, as people. Trust builds empathy, understanding, shared commitment, mutual obligation, integrity, and collective responsibility. Top-down accountability should be used only as a last resort when trust and collective responsibility have collapsed.

One of the most important tasks of leadership is building trust in a community through repeated, deliberate, and considerate actions. Building trust is slow. It takes time. A little trust is followed by greater trust, then complete trust. Trust isn't innocent or blind. It grows when the evidence of its results is demonstrated day after day, year upon year.

It's hard enough to build and maintain trust as a leader. It's an immense challenge to accomplish it as a system. So, what does a trust-based, rather than accountability-driven, system look like, in practice? Where does *Leadership From the Middle* contribute to and become part of a trust-based system? For some clues, let's turn to the highly regarded educational system of Finland.

Finnish educational specialist, Professor Pasi Sahlberg, knows his country and its educational system inside-out. The son of a teacher, Sahlberg taught mathematics as a young man, and went on to be responsible for professional development in Finland's Ministry of Education in the 1990s. When the first ever results of the OECD's PISA tests of 15-year-olds' performance in reading, mathematics, and science were published in 2000, and Finland stunned the world by turning out to be the top performer, Sahlberg suddenly became his nation's interlocutor. Highly placed in the Finnish educational system, fluent in English, and with a PhD in teaching and educational change, Sahlberg became the world's go-to person on the reasons for Finland's educational success.

Sahlberg carried his message worldwide through his work with transnational organizations like the World Bank in the early 2000s. After publishing several research papers, he went on to write the definitive book on Finland's education success and what it meant for everyone else – *Finnish Lessons.*[3]

Many of the reasons for Finland's success have since become well known and are widely talked about. Teaching in Finland is a highly valued profession – second only to medicine when looking for potential husbands, and absolute top when looking for wives, for example – and all teachers have master's degrees. Collaboration among teachers is encouraged, routine, and occurs during the school day where teachers have more time scheduled out of class than teachers in any other nation. For children and young people, the curriculum is not overcrowded, teachers have high autonomy to develop their own programmes of study, and there is no high-stakes testing. Schools are part of a strongly funded public system, almost everyone places their children within that public system, and there is an overall commitment to strong communities and public life.

In 2006, I was invited by the OECD to join a team of four to investigate how school leadership in Finland contributed to the country's educational success.[4] Our report was one of the first narratives about Finnish education from outside the country. We saw a system where teachers elected their school leaders who then didn't really have a mandate to drive teachers through making changes that they weren't interested in. We saw a system that had abolished its inspection service in favour of investing in teachers. We heard officials say that if principals were performing badly, under excessive stress, or were even alcoholics (Finland has one of the highest levels of alcohol abuse in the world!), they didn't punish the principals or fire them from their jobs – they simply helped them instead. Last, we saw municipalities operate from a principle of subsidiarity – moving as much power and decision-making control to the people who were closest to where those decisions would be exercised, and closest to who would be most affected.

Pasi Sahlberg and Timothy Walker, an American teaching in Finland, have one word to sum up a lot of what we recorded in our report: *trust*.[5] Finland, they note, comes out at or very near the top of several global rankings of trust and corporate transparency. It is an equitable if rather homogeneous society, with lower levels of economic inequality than most of the rest of the developed world. This means that elites and non-elites alike are not consumed by envy and competition, and believe, together, in the value of public services and welfare. But Sahlberg and Walker explain that trust in schools isn't just a by-product of these wider beliefs and dispositions. Teachers in school, they explain, are the second most trusted profession after the police. Even in the land of the trusting and the trusted, teachers turn out to be accorded higher levels of trust than almost anyone else. Trust in schools, in other words, doesn't ooze from the pores of the Finnish people as if they all lived in some moral or spiritual sauna. It's a result of deliberate policy.

In 1991, the authors explain, there was a banking collapse. This placed huge pressure on the government to dramatically reduce public spending. In part, but only in part, Finland followed the path of other nations at the time that moved away from central government control towards more decentralized models of administration. But the similarity stopped there. Unlike the United Kingdom, United States, Chile, and Sweden, Finland did not introduce semi-private systems of school competition. Decentralization did not leave everyone to fend for themselves. Rather, citing an earlier paper co-written by Sahlberg, the authors note that "the culture of trust . . . was introduced because local authorities did not want central bureaucrats making the difficult financial decisions that would affect their children and schools".[6]

Moreover, the Finnish government abandoned centralized textbooks, avoided high-stakes testing, and got rid of the school inspection system, all to save costs. Instead, Finland invested in its teachers. It didn't pick the highest academic performers for the education profession, but it made teaching very hard to get into, with applicants needing to show prior evidence of commitment to working with young people, often in a voluntary capacity. The master's degrees were the credentialled icing on this moral and professional cake. Instead of implementing a standardized curriculum, teachers in every school across the land were involved in planning curriculum locally, in their own municipalities. There was no separation between a curriculum conceived by bureaucrats at the head of the system that then had to be executed by teachers at the foot of it. By developing curriculum and pedagogy at the same time, teachers brought conception and execution, head, hand, and heart, together. In place of top-down tests, new teachers developed sophisticated skills in assessment for learning. The overall result was that not only did educators trust each other's judgements, but the public trusted teachers' judgements too. And the consequences became very clear in the nation's high performance in relation to its global counterparts.

In schools themselves, trust doesn't happen naturally. It's developed quite deliberately. Sahlberg and Walker show how giving children ascending levels of trust depends on scaffolding degrees of trust – and risk – in their own lives, to travel independently through the neighbourhood, manage their own time, and use sharp tools without close supervision. Trust is about building competence as well as relationships. This is not earned trust – giving trust only to a small elite of schools or professionals on condition that they have achieved excellent results. Trust is not a privilege. It is a human right – at least until that trust has been seriously broken by cheating, theft, violence, or abuse.

In 2013–2014, Petri Salbo and Torbjorn Sanden administered a survey on trust to almost 600 teachers and principals who mainly belonged to the Swedish speaking minority, in Finnish schools. The three highest ranked statements by respondents were:[7]

- Government policies support quality public education for all, regardless of family income.
- Quality teaching is one of the educational system's highest priorities.
- Teacher unions are an agency for school improvement in the school system and schools.

This is what a trust-based system looks like, and the results are plain to see. It's certainly a direction for other systems to follow – highly professionalized teachers who work together designing their own curriculum in collaboration with each other, for the learners they know best, within and across their schools. It's an embedded and ingrained way to *Lead From the Middle*.

But is it transferable to societies and systems that have key differences from Finnish culture and politics? Finland remains a rather homogeneous society united by the presence of a somewhat unfriendly power on the other side of its eastern border. It is a high tax economy with relatively stronger levels of public investment than the low tax economies of the United States and United Kingdom, for example. Its policy was not a gradual and evolutionary development, but a response to an existential threat. There is continuity of support for public education across Finland's political parties, from one government to the next, rather than a vulnerability to shifts and swings in government priorities every four or five years.

In aspirational terms, Finland's education model still has a lot to offer other nations, especially those characterized by relative government stability. All nations everywhere should look to Finland to dial back as much as they can from the bureaucratic restrictions of top-down control, and the devastating consequences of cut-throat competition. Even so, as an overall blueprint for change, a trust-based model of *Leadership From the Middle* is harder to transpose to nations with greater levels of inequality, more turbulent politics, and higher levels of racial and ethnic diversity. So, what other paths are there instead?

Self-Improving School Systems

What is the opposite of Finnish collectivism and ingrained trust? One answer is autocracy – the very thing that Finns have opposed. But there is another opposite, as well. Anarchy. UK professor David Hargreaves is not an unabashed anarchist, but he turns to anarchist theory and practice for inspiration. He makes this very clear in the subtitle of his 2019 book, *Beyond Schooling: An Anarchist Challenge.*[8]

David Hargreaves is not my brother, my partner, or my father. We are not related at all. But we have known each other for almost 50 years. I had the privilege of working with David for three years when I was a lecturer at Oxford University in the 1980s. We had offices next door to each other, team-taught graduate classes together, and brainstormed and battled with ideas on long walks across the university's parks. David is one of the greatest intellectuals in education I have ever known. He revels in counterintuitive, even contrarian thinking, sometimes for its own sake. Fittingly, his kind of anarchy would not fit most people's perceptions or prejudices. He is anarchic even in his relation to anarchy.

In *Beyond Schooling*, Hargreaves criticizes the constant march from the mid 1970s onwards of ever-tightening state control over schools – right down to the details of curriculum content, standardized testing, and top-down inspection systems. England moved from being one of the least to one of the most centralized systems in the world, he argues. Semi-autonomous educational bodies responsible for curriculum, technology, and leadership like the *National College for School Leadership*, and *the Specialist Schools and Academies Trust*, were all abolished or placed under direct government control. Ministers and civil servants assumed immense powers even over the details of classroom practice. Whether it is governed by the political Left or Right, Hargreaves argues, the state tightens surveillance and control, "damages spontaneous self-organization", and either obstructs innovation or incorporates "any innovations into itself, in order to control them".[9]

Hargreaves's reference to spontaneous self-organization provides a clue about his distinctive interpretation of anarchism. Anarchism, for Hargreaves, is not that of the individual libertarian who seeks freedom from all control and regulation, wherever it originates. It is not disruption for its own sake. Instead, Hargreaves proposes a more communalist (not communist!) view of anarchy that is rooted in the belief that, as far as possible, communities should be able to look after their own affairs and take care of themselves without government interference. Mutual aid and support of the kind that characterizes craft guilds, rather than external regulation, create and support independence and originality. In this version of anarchism, communities govern themselves through the "self-government of the smaller commune" rather than being subject to "the exercise of power" by a "ruling and dominant minority".[10]

Hargreaves is pessimistic about the possibilities for achieving educational transformation through tightly coordinated state policy, whether it is Left or Right in orientation. Instead, he proposes an anarchist alternative that puts people at the centre of being able to help themselves through association and cooperation. Hargreaves expresses this anarchist principle through three examples.

First is a belief in the power of *homeschooling*, of doing away with large aspects of schools as institutions altogether. His views here harken back to the de-schooling movements of the 1970s. The experience of COVID-19, however, suggests that Hargreaves was overoptimistic about the potential of homeschooling to bring about widespread change.[11] Remote learning during COVID-19 worked best for privileged families with strong networks of support and expertise or for students who were no longer susceptible to bullying. But, in most families, mothers who had to assume disproportionate responsibility for supervising their children's learning at home found it almost impossible to manage their own careers at the same time. One of the age-old reasons children need to be in public schools is custody. Schools are places where children go so their parents can work. It's not the only reason, but it remains a very powerful one.

Second, Hargreaves discusses changes at the periphery of systems "where exciting innovative practice flourishes".[12] As we have seen in Tom Hatch's analysis of these kinds of innovations, they do offer some promise, and throw up new ideas that can go mainstream. But most innovative schools and networks remain outliers of or safety valves for unchanged systems rather than being part of a system change that can benefit everyone.

Last, but not least, is what Hargreaves, following an obscure government education memorandum in England in 2006, calls a *self-improving school system* (SISS).[13] This idea has gained a lot of traction among academics and school administrators in England, but it has not yet spread much to systems in other parts of the world.

A SISS is built around clusters of schools that work together to develop local solutions under system leadership. With the evolution of networked systems of organization, there is potential for some aspects of SISS to combine innovation with systemwide change. However, in 2018, professors Toby Greany and Rob Higham, whose research I reported earlier, presented the results of their detailed and systematic analysis of what SISS looked like in practice and of whether it was achieving its ideal.[14] They interviewed 164 educators in 47 schools, along with 18 policy makers and system-leaders. They also surveyed almost 700 school leaders across the country. What did they conclude?

To begin with, the English educational system, of which SISS was regarded as being an integral part, was made up of three elements:

- *A tightly controlling top-down regime* of inspection, standardization, testing, and results-related funding.
- *School-by-school competition* for student numbers and for students whose backgrounds might predict greater potential for academic success, in a system of school choice where performance results and brand advantage became key factors.
- *Pressures, incentives, and inducements for schools to participate in collaborative systems of help and support* to develop new practices, to seek help when they were underperforming, and, if they were high performing themselves, to lead others by offering them assistance.

David Hargreaves's anarchist ideals are strongly rooted in the third possibility of lateral support and deeply opposed to the first factor of top-down control. Hargreaves is less expansive, though, about the threats to SISS of unleashed market competition, which was already building up a head of steam when he began developing his ideas.

Much of the rest of Greany's and Higham's report examines what happens to lateral collaboration that is at the root of SISS when it operates within a system that is also characterized by market competition and top-down control. There is:

- *Incoherence* of a chaotic system of local authority (district) schools along with various kinds of independent academies in different kinds and sizes of chains and trusts. In the words of one interviewee, "'System' implies that there's a good degree of articulate design. And I think what's happening nationally is that there are all sorts of systems . . . So, there isn't really *a system*, and . . . nobody knows what works".[15]
- *Diminishing support* due to overall austerity policies and to strategies to reduce local authority funding so as to strengthen central government control and exert increased pressure on schools to join the market system of academies instead.
- *Distraction* of energies in schools towards improved branding, entrepreneurialism, and developing fee-for-service curriculum development and professional learning services to enhance school budgets.
- *Cooption* of "elite" and especially "charismatic, authoritarian" leaders of multiple schools, as well as their own, who become complicit with dubious government policies and who also become self-aggrandizing in how they accrue personal and organizational benefits from their efforts.[16]
- *Destruction of place and community* when teachers, parents, and other stakeholders are not "allowed to participate and have a representative voice in decisions over the restructuring of local school systems".[17]

In practice, as Hargreaves and other SISS analysts concede, neoliberal governments have hijacked the self-help narrative to justify austerity policies that reduce or withdraw vital supports for state schools. At one point in his book, Hargreaves draws on the work of William Godwin, the father of the famed Gothic author, Mary Shelley, and his advocacy for anarchism.[18] Ironically, it seems, the early optimism of SISS may have created another Shelley-like Frankenstein that is destroying its communitarian-loving masters with unbridled market competition and tyrannies of top-down control. To conclude, although statism is often excessively constraining, in a starkly unequal society, the alternative of cooperative anarchism is too easily exploited for market-driven ends.

University of Pennsylvania professor, Jonathan Supovitz, is less pessimistic. In his attempt to help US educators make sense of the convoluted system of education in England, he has hopes that Americans can learn how to build an effective middle tier of educational administration. "How can educators in the US extricate themselves from bureaucratic oppression and lateral isolation?", he asks.[19] Responding to his own question, he argues that "the American system would benefit from a formal expansion of leadership positions in schools from the traditional reliance on a strong single actor with a weak supporting cast, towards a more deliberately integrated system of school leadership".[20] There are many educators and researchers who would doubtless agree with him. But, if the English experience is anything to go by, this way of rethinking *Leadership From the Middle* will only turn out positively if American policy makers are willing to abandon their addiction to privatized competition and top-down control.

Social Movements

SISS and educational networks may not always be innovative, equitable, or inclusive. They may too easily accept government parameters of policies that are harmful to students such as win-lose parental competition among schools, high-stakes standardized tests, or indiscriminate adoptions of digital learning technologies. How we can we be confident that SISS aren't innovative for their own sake, and don't benefit privileged schools more than others? How can SISS become truly transformative in an inclusive, humanistic, and equitable way?

One answer can be found in the idea of social movements. Social movements are grounded in senses of moral purpose and commitment that are meant to benefit everyone. As British author, Peter Byrne, argues, "[s]ocial movements are expressive in that they have beliefs and moral principles and they seek to persuade everyone – governments, parents, the general public, anyone who will listen – that these values are the right ones".[21] Social movements challenge and resist prevailing ways of governing that serve elite and privileged interests. They are evident in the labour movement, in environmental movements of climate change activism, in the women's and #MeToo movements, and in the global influence of Black Lives Matter.

Social movements are also evident in education. Dennis Shirley's research on community organizing in education has shown how the Alliance Schools in Texas in the 1990s mobilized parents of marginalized children to focus on and secure quick wins together as part of a longer-term struggle for equity and inclusion.[22] Social movements from below can be a powerful strategy for bringing about transformational change in education outside conventional state mechanisms of top-down implementation.

In *Liberating Learning: Educational Change as Social Movement*, Santiago Rincon-Gallardo examines powerful examples of systemwide transformation in the Global South that have been achieved through social movement principles.[23] Global policy rhetoric has asserted that countries in the Global South can only improve with top-down strategies of curriculum prescription, implementation targets, and standardized testing because they typically have weak teacher capacity. Against this view, Rincon-Gallardo describes large-scale changes that have achieved measurable improvements by identifying and moving around the knowledge and capacities that teachers already possess, rather than imposing programmes to compensate for capacities these teachers supposedly lack.

One example is the *Escuela Nueva* group of over 20,000 rural schools that is rooted in but has expanded far beyond Colombia. In a system that has grown over 40 years, these schools have not only outperformed comparable schools in conventional achievement in Latin America, according to World Bank data.[24] They have also transformed pedagogy in ways that build on and cohere with the foundational ideas of John Dewey, Paulo Freire, and Maria Montessori. They focus the curriculum on pursuing transformational goals of securing peace, democracy, and connection to local rural environments, in part by involving students in school governance. These values define the movement, continue to be advocated globally by Escuela Nueva's inspirational and multi-award-winning co-founder, Vicky Colbert, and they motivate teachers to respond to the needs of their local communities. In a case study of Escuela Nueva, Michael O'Connor and I reported how transformational practices are developed and circulated through demonstration lessons in local teachers' centres that teachers ride over the mountains on their motorcycles to witness and discuss.[25] Escuela Nueva is not just a network of a few dozen or even a few hundred schools outside the mainstream. It is a movement that is changing the world.

An educational movement that is closer to home for me is the ARC Education Collaboratory that was mentioned earlier.[26] Started in 2016, in collaboration with my Norwegian colleague, Yngve Lindvig, this movement began as a counter to established transnational organizations, and to national policy systems that were still preoccupied with testing and technology. ARC is a group of countries serving democracies and it is about democracies that promote human rights. Before COVID-19, it met at an annual summit to engage with local schools, be stimulated by internationally regarded thought leaders who also donated their time for free, and work in facilitated groups of trusted peers who coached each other on significant problems of policy together. During COVID-19, ARC's work continued virtually every two months and addressed compelling issues that systems were dealing with during the pandemic, such as well-being, learning outdoors, and high school examinations.

As a result of being in ARC, systems have changed their policies on well-being, provided outdoor learning spaces for every elementary school, rethought high school examinations, and upgraded the priority they give to vocational education. Even so, most social movements eventually outgrow themselves. They surpass their purpose, the changes become embedded, and people move on. The point of them in *Leadership From the Middle* is to get large numbers of people to move towards a trust-based educational system that can be a self-improving system too. It is to move from networks and collaboratives to movements and self-improving systems that can respond to the forces that are assailing us in our crisis-driven world with socially just solutions that fit the communities that educators know best. As Tom Hatch indicated, it's unlikely that such movements, like other attempts at transformation, will be successful in an unsympathetic social system that is totalitarian in nature, bureaucratic in its habits, or profoundly unequal economically. In unconducive systems such as these, educational movements will have little success unless they are also a part of and connected to wider social movements. We must change schools if we want to change the world and we must change the world if we want to transform our schools in an equitable and inclusive way.

Conclusion

The turbulence of the world is not going to stop. Things are going to keep on flying in all directions. The Big Five omni-crisis will affect our work for many years to come. We must educate young people to get engaged with this world, believe they can have an impact, and develop the knowledge and skills to do so. This calls for leadership, but not any kind of leadership. Leaders must understand the big picture but be close to the action. They must know where their students are, in every respect, no matter what kind of community they are in. We need lots of leaders everywhere, not just one or two at the top. This *Leadership From the Middle* is leadership from a systemic middle, from a place where collaboration is key, networks are imperative, and people can move positive change forward together – in equity, well-being, inclusion, democracy, and human rights. It is also a moral middle, where leaders have a clear moral compass, are not defeated by obstacles, and are not distracted by glittery but ethically questionable projects and initiatives.

Leadership From the Middle means doing good and being good. It doesn't mean being perfect or having to know everything and be everywhere all at once. But it does mean collaborating with others for the common benefit of all young people, especially those that the system has served badly up to now. It does mean taking collective responsibility for each other's improvement. And it does mean robust networking for a clear purpose, and not just for the transient joy that the process can bring.

Leaders who need to make headway at the top aren't and mustn't be nullified by *Leadership From the Middle*. Their role is to set the overall direction, inspire commitment and action, and provide the resources and supports so those closer to the middle can make things happen together; so that they can develop policies and not just implement them. And people at the foot of the system have a part to play too. Most of the best new practices in schools began not in a psychology laboratory, or in a central bureaucracy, but in a teacher's classroom somewhere. What emerges at the very frontlines of education should not only spread to others. It should also cohere with the moral direction in which the system is moving. That is the point of *Leadership From the Middle*.

It is especially when things are going badly, when great wrongs are occurring, that all of us can play a part. In 1980, 16,000 workers at the Gdansk shipyard in Poland went on strike when Anna Walentynowicz, a labour activist, was fired from her job. The gruelling strike led to the Polish Solidarity movement that involved millions, and that eventually hastened the collapse of the Berlin Wall that changed the world forever. "I was the drop that caused the cup of bitterness to overflow", Walentynowicz reflected.[27]

Leadership From the Middle is not a set of roles, positions, tasks, and responsibilities. Nor is it just a mediating layer, level, or tier of something else. It is the beating heart of educational transformation. It can and should involve anyone and everyone in building something better together, including you.

If you find yourself somewhere in the middle, don't follow the lyric of Maurice and Barry Gibb of the Bee Gees and be the "fool of a man (or woman) in the middle of a complicated plan" – someone who's lost, who doesn't get or make the big picture, who is just a connector or a cog in an incomprehensible machine and who doesn't know which way to turn.[28] Be a leader, make some change, and find a diverse group of friends and allies to do that with. That is what *Leadership From the Middle* is ultimately all about.

EPILOGUE
YOUR LEADERSHIP

What does it take to be a leader who is at the very centre, at the very core, in the beating heart of educational change and improvement? What does it require to transform learning and teaching and face down the Big Five that are coming after us?

We will need to devote more attention to the well-being of children and adults alike so that everyone can feel safe and thrive.[1] We will also need to help our young people think harder about war and peace, the environment, democracy, and inclusion. There's also a huge opportunity to transform many aspects of how our school systems work. Learning from the best examples of governments that responded with the greatest agility and integrity to the pandemic, we can develop policy and strategy in education much more collaboratively among ministers, senior system leaders, school districts, teachers, school leaders, students, and parents. We can lead together from the middle, rather than scurrying around to implement mandates that come down from the top, or than floundering around in chaos in communities that have no local organizations to pull everything together.

The threats of the Big Five are real. They will not be going away soon, if ever. There is good reason to be afraid, of course. But none of us can lead from positions of fear. We must face our threats and fears together and empower our students and ourselves to respond to them. We must do this by developing curriculum and assessment processes that equip all our young people with the knowledge, skills, and mentalities to become agents of change and improvement in

    DOI: 10.4324/9781315682921-8

their lives, no matter what jobs or careers they take up. We must also build inclusive, collaborative, and empowered systems that pull everyone together in a common cause to serve the public good, rather than tearing them apart by feeding the basic instincts of win-lose competition.

Many obstacles will impede us. But these obstacles are already becoming our ways – to connect learning more to nature, completely rethink assessments, give young people active experiences of democracy, and address the needs of the whole child. Constant disruptions by wars, weather events, and other Big Five manifestations of the omni-crisis will distract us. But we must not be tempted to turn to the false certainties of unethical bad leaders to try and save us. Utopias of perfection are an illusion. Zero achievement gaps are a delusion. Flawlessly perfect leadership is unattainable and undesirable. We've all got our own imperfections. But together, we can overcome obstacles, get past them, and sometimes work with them to make our schools more equitable and inclusive. We can change the world by thinking and leading organically in how we develop our young people and how we change our schools – connecting the head, heart, and hand (and feet) in every learner, and every system. Let's put the mechanical age of top-down change behind us. Let's develop a sustainable system of *Leadership From the Middle* that is responsive to our diverse communities and students instead.

To close, here are seven ways that you and other educators who want to *Lead From the Middle* can do exactly that:

1. Lead Off

Don't wait for others to take the initiative. Your prime directive is not just to implement initiatives. It's to seize the initiative yourself. If you see something needs doing, don't wait for others to go first. You may be the one everyone is looking to. Forgiveness is easier to ask for than permission. Proceed until apprehended. If you're close to the foot of the action, you will see issues emerging long before people at the top notice, long before researchers have drawn attention to it, and long before policy makers decide to do something about it. So don't be afraid to lead off, to be the first to make a move. You'll be surprised how quickly others around you will show they have noticed things too and will be more than willing to follow your lead.

2. Lead Up

In his 2021 business book, *Leading From the Middle*, Scott Mautz sets out numerous mindsets and skillsets for leaders who find themselves somewhere in the middle. One of the most compelling is "Leading Your Boss".[2] I think of this as leading up. Leaders who find themselves in the hierarchical middle of their organizations often think about how to implement things from the top, percolate things up from the bottom, and network with peers and colleagues laterally. They rarely think about leading up. When your boss calls you in, what's your first response? Most people to whom I put this question respond with "Uh! Oh!" or "What have I done now?" But if you lead up and see that the obstacle that is your boss is really your way to accomplish things that matter to you, the conversation can turn out totally differently. What if you think, "I have a few precious minutes with the boss! What purpose can I advance? What resources can I get? Who can I advocate for? How can I give the boss some unsolicited positive feedback – something bosses very rarely get? How can I use this conversation to drive a change forward that will benefit everyone?" This is not just about connecting the system's dots up, following a direction, or acting as a bridge in the middle. It's about genuinely leading *from* the middle.

3. Lead Through Paradox

When you're in the middle, you can sometimes feel Janus-faced. Janus was the Roman god who presided over archways, gates, and doors. His head had to look both ways at the same time. This can feel like another obstacle of *Leadership From the Middle*. Middle leaders, as educational researchers have found, often feel that they serve two masters, are constantly pulled in opposite directions, and can feel conflicted and overwhelmed as a result.[3] But once again, the obstacle can become the way. The opposites can be converted into a paradox of opposite truths that require resolution and finessing with pragmatism, creativity, and artistry. Take, for example, the second of Kristiansen's 11 paradoxes of management that I discussed in Chapter 2: the paradox of having to take the lead *and* recede into the background. On the one hand, leaders mustn't become insufferable by always hogging the limelight. But they can't stand back so much that no one realizes who is in charge, or where the inspiration is going to come from. Being in the middle is riddled with paradox but not necessarily in a bad way. *Leadership From the Middle* involves being able to hold together opposing truths in the service of a higher moral imperative, and to know when and how to balance them, integrate them, and sometimes break through by finding a third path beyond them that no one else has thought of yet.

4. Lead Together

Wherever you are in leadership, you cannot lead everything yourself, all the time. In a complex and constantly changing environment, many heads are better than one, and all hands need to be on deck. Leaders need to be able to draw people in and bring them together. This means far more than assigning tasks, roles, and responsibilities. *Leadership From the Middle* means building collective responsibility for each other's success in the service of a greater good. It means knowing how to network with people far away as well as developing trust with colleagues close at hand. Leaders who lead from the middle need to know how to motivate, support, and challenge everyone around them to be better and do better and to promote change that will improve learning and well-being for everyone. *Leadership From the Middle* is not about being paid for added responsibilities. It is about assuming moral and professional responsibility with others to bring about improvements and transformations that benefit everyone.

5. Lead Inclusively

Networks tend to attract people who like to network. So do network leaders. These might be people who embrace change, enjoy novelty, and love to interact. Networkers are often extroverts. They are what

Manuel Kets De Vries, in his book on the psychiatry of leadership, *The Leader on the Couch*, calls dramatics. Dramatics are often effective in the middle of organizations, he says. They generate excitement, often give initiatives and their brand an attractive and positive appeal, and they stimulate interactions and connections among others. Dramatics are "very likeable with considerable charm and enthusiasm which makes other people initially want to work for them".[4] They are less effective "in situations where performance is measured by competence, diligence, thoroughness and depth". They are not so good at seeing things through, getting workaday things like budgets done, collaborating with others of a different disposition, and persuading more cautious policy makers to change. Also, when things don't go their way, they are prone to become, well – dramatic! In her bestselling book, *Quiet*, Susan Cain points out that over 50 per cent of Americans identify as introverts.[5] Many introverts are like my wife, Pauline. They dread Halloween, can't stand icebreakers, and are opposed to making exhibitions of themselves. In networks or other ways of *Leadership From the Middle*, we need to make sure we work with diversity from the outset. We cannot lead from the middle if we are all extroverts, or white men (or white women for that matter), or if we turn systems of leadership into self-preserving gerontocracies or self-perpetuating oligarchies. We can't just lead for inclusion. We must also lead through inclusion, so that we are diverse in identities, expertise, and perspectives. In that way, we can get closer to all the people whom we serve.

6. Lead Sustainably

Plan for your own obsolescence. Do not take up everyone else's oxygen. Move to the front when you must, but do not personify being the hub of everything. Share the load. Share the stage. Distribute work that you love doing and not just work you'd be glad to dispose of. Make sure you are creating a culture and a system where, before too long, many people would be able to step into your shoes at any time. Support other people's networks and contacts that will benefit their careers as well as advancing the network contacts that will benefit you. Don't imagine project funding will last forever.

Either make sure what you are doing gets embedded into the policy or financial system or be very clear about what you are learning that will outlast the entity you are leading now.

7. Lead for Good

You can't lead forever. But you should lead for good. Never let gilt-edged opportunities blind you to your moral purpose. Choose your funding partners wisely. Stay focused on your mission and on the people whom you serve, whether you feel everything is going for or against you. Look for when the obstacle might be the way. Communicate to your colleagues the tiniest steps that have been achieved in reaching your goals. Share the big picture, so others can feel they are involved in an epic journey with you. Many indigenous communities believe that self-transcendence is even more basic to our hierarchies of need than food or shelter. *Leadership From the Middle* for good will sometimes require sacrifice of money, time, energy, and other priorities. This happens in most social movements. Yet with the sacrifice comes accomplishment, service to others, and considerable companionship and joy. This is the good you do for others. And that is the greatness you must try and discover within yourself.

Sources

Some of the contents of this book draw on work I have previously published individually, or with co-authors, reproduced in adapted form, here, with customary permission of the publishers and co-authors concerned to reuse contents of published articles in extended works of my own.

The research on Ontario school districts, which ultimately inspired this book and on which much of the material in Chapters 4 and 5 is based, was first presented in two technical research reports on the projects. They are: Hargreaves, A., Braun, H.I., Hughes, M., Chapman, L., Lam, K., Lee, Y., Morton, B., Sallis, K., Steiner, A., & Welch, M. (2012) *Leading for all: A research report on the development, design, implementation, and impact of Ontario's "Essential for some, good for all" initiative*, Ontario: Council of Directors of Education; and Hargreaves, A., Shirley, D., Wangia, S., Bacon, C., & D'Angelo, M. (2018) *Leading from the middle*, Ontario: Council of Directors of Education.

An earlier effort to analyse the concept of *Leading From the Middle* was first presented in a journal article, co-authored with my colleague and project co-principal investigator, Dennis Shirley, in 2019. Material from this paper is reproduced and also developed and expanded in edited form here. See Hargreaves, A., & Shirley, D. (2020) Leading from the middle: Its nature, origins and importance,

Journal of Professional Capital and Community 5(1): 92–114, https://doi.org/10.1108/JPCC-06-2019-0013

My work and thinking on networks have been greatly influenced by collaborating with Dr Danette Parsley who, at the time of our research with rural school networks in the US Pacific Northwest, was leading the development project for the Northwest Comprehensive Centre. In particular, the six principles of network development outlined in Chapter 6 (of which Dr Parsley is a co-author) were first discussed in an earlier form in an article written collaboratively with her and with Boston College graduate student at the time, Elizabeth Cox. See Hargreaves, A., Parsley, D., & Cox, E. (2015) Designing and launching rural school improvement networks: Aspirations and actualities, *Peabody Journal of Education* 90(2): 306–321.

An earlier version of the material that opens Chapter 1 first appeared in Hargreaves, A., & Shirley, D. (2021) Deep engagement and broad well-being, *Principal Connections* 25(2): 10–13.

Other parts of this book draw on and sometimes reproduce or adapt smaller extracts from previous papers or chapters.

A section on autonomy and transparency in Chapter 2 draws on Hargreaves, A. (2015) Autonomy and transparency: Two good ideas gone bad, in Evers, J., & Kneber, R. (Eds) *Flip the system*, New York: Routledge, pp. 120–133.

An earlier description of the school-to-school cross-district collaboration in the Greater Manchester Challenge appears in Hargreaves, A., & Ainscow, M. (2015) The top and bottom of leadership and change, *Phi Delta Kappan* 97(3): 42–48. Curiously, we titled this article "Leading from the middle", but the journal publisher substituted the version they finally went with.

Some parts of the final chapter were first thought through in a paper that was stimulated by and sprang from the work of Karen Seashore Louis on innovation and knowledge dissemination. See Hargreaves, A. (2022) High school change: A reflective essay on three decades of frustration, struggle and progress, *Journal of Educational Administration* 60(3): 245–261, https://doi.org/10.1108/JEA-01-2022-0013

Two forewords I have written for colleagues' books in the field have provided material for parts of this book. In Chapter 1, my discussion of imperfect leadership draws on my foreword to Munby, S., &

Bretherton, M.-C. (2022) *Imperfect leadership in action*, Carmarthen: Crown House Publishing, and the section on trust-based systems in Chapter 6 draws on my foreword to Sahlberg, P., & Walker, T.D. (2021) *In teachers we trust*, New York: W.W. Norton.

My short description of the life and work of Seymour Sarason in Chapter 1 first appeared as part of a biographical chapter on Sarason in Hargreaves, A. (2001) Seymour B. Sarason, in Palmer, J. (Ed.) *50 modern thinkers on education: From Piaget to the present*, London: Routledge/Falmer Press, pp. 133–141.

Occasional references to the leadership implications of the COVID-19 pandemic in this book are partly based on my contributing chapter to a Royal Society of Canada online report on COVID-19 and schools: Hargreaves, A. (2021) What the COVID-19 pandemic has taught us about teachers and teaching, in Vaillancourt, T. (Ed.) *Children and schools during Covid-19 and beyond: Engagement and connection through opportunity*, Ottawa: Royal Society of Canada.

Notes

Preface

1 Hargreaves, A., & Fink, D. (2006) *Sustainable leadership*, San Francisco: Wiley.
2 Hargreaves, A., & Fink, D. (2022) Sustainable leadership in a post-pandemic world, *ICP Magazine*, August, pp 5–12, https://www.andyhargreaves.com/uploads/5/2/9/2/5292616/icp-august-magazine-2022-final-1_ah.pdf
3 Hargreaves, A., Braun, H.I., Hughes, M., Chapman, L., Lam, K., Lee, Y., Morton, B., Sallis, K., Steiner, A., & Welch, M. (2012) *Leading for all: A research report on the development, design, implementation, and impact of Ontario's "Essential for some, good for all" initiative*, Ontario: Council of Directors of Education.
4 Hargreaves, A. (2020) Large-scale assessments and their effects: The case of mid-stakes tests in Ontario, *Journal of Educational Change*, 21: 393–420, https://doi.org/10.1007/s10833-020-09380-5; Shirley, D., Hargreaves, A., & Washington, S. (2020) The sustainability and non-sustainability of teachers' and leaders' wellbeing, *Teaching and Teacher Education*, March, https://doi.org/10.1016/j.tate.2019.102987; Hargreaves, A., & Shirley, D. (2020) Leading from the middle: Its nature, origins and importance, *Journal of Professional Capital and Community* 5(1): 92–114, https://doi.org/10.1108/JPCC-06-2019-0013
5 Hargreaves, A., Shirley, D., Wangia, S., Bacon, C., & D'Angelo, M. (2018) *Leading from the middle*, Ontario. Council of Directors of Education.
6 Hargreaves, A., Halasz, G., & Pont, B. (2008) The Finnish approach to system leadership, in Pont, B., Nusche, D., & Hopkins, D. (Eds) *Improving school leadership, volume 2, case studies on system leadership*, Paris: OECD,

pp. 69–109; Hargreaves, A. (2014) Building the professional capital for schools to deliver successful change, in *Improving schools in Wales*, Paris: OECD, pp. 64–90; Hargreaves, A. (2015) Schooling, teachers and leadership, in *Improving schools in Scotland*, Paris: OECD, pp. 115–144.

7 Hargreaves, A., & Ainscow, M. (2015) The top and bottom of leadership and change, *Phi Delta Kappan*, November, pp. 42–48.

8 Hargreaves, A., Parsley, D., & Cox, E. (2015) Designing and launching rural school improvement networks: Aspirations and actualities, *Peabody Journal of Education* 90(2): 306–321.

9 www.playjouer.ca

10 www.atrico.org

11 Hargreaves, D.H. (2019) *Beyond schooling: An anarchist challenge*, London: Routledge.

12 Hargreaves, A. (2022) High school change: A reflective essay on three decades of frustration, struggle and progress, *Journal of Educational Administration* 60(3): 245–261, https://doi.org/10.1108/JEA-01-2022-0013

Chapter 1: Looking for Our Leaders

1 The number of five million was reported during COVID-19. Official cases reported to the World Health Organization exceeded 6.5 million as of November 2022. See https://covid19.who.int/. These numbers exclude higher estimates based on changes in excess death rates during the pandemic in which many of these excess deaths have been attributed to the direct and indirect effects of COVID-19.

2 UNESCO (2020) *COVID-19 impact on education*, https://en.unesco.org/covid19/educationresponse

3 World Health Organization (2018) Managing epidemics: Key facts about major deadly diseases, p. 11, https://www.who.int/emergencies/diseases/managing-epidemics-interactive.pdf

4 Hickman, C., Marks, E., Pihkala, P., Clayton, S., Lewandowski, R.E., Mayall, E.E., Wray, B., Mellor, C., & Van Susteren, L. (2021) Young people's voices on climate anxiety, government betrayal and moral injury: A global phenomenon, *The Lancet*, https://papers.ssrn.com/sol3/papers.cfm?abstract_id=3918955

5 International Committee of the Red Cross (2019) Majority of millennials see catastrophic war as real possibility, and believe there should be limits, 16 January, https://www.icrc.org/en/document/majority-millennials-see-catastrophic-war-real-possibility

6 Strom, M.S. (1994) *Facing history and ourselves: Holocaust and human behavior*, Brookline: National Foundation, p. xiv.

7 The Economist Intelligence Unit (2021) *Democracy index 2020: In sickness and in health?* London, https://www.eiu.com/n/campaigns/democracy-index-2020/

8 Tinline, P. (2022) The authoritarian interlude: How can politicians win back voters who have become disillusioned with parliamentary democracy? *New Statesman*, 4 August. https://www.newstatesman.com/ideas/2022/08/the-authoritarian-interlude

9 United Nations (2022) Youth Declaration on Transforming Education, *Transforming Education Summit,* New York City, September. https://www.un.org/sites/un2.un.org/files/2022/09/tes_youthdeclaration_en.pdf

10 World Bank (2021) Urgent, effective action required to quell the impact of COVID-19 on education worldwide, worldbank.org/en/news/immersive-story/2021/01/22/urgent-effective-action-required-to-quell-the-impact-of-covid-19-on-education-worldwide; Economist Leader (2020) The risks of keeping schools closed far outweigh the benefits, *The Economist*, economist.com/leaders/2020/07/18/the-risks-of-keeping-schools-closed-far-outweigh-the-benefits; Finn, C. (2020) How badly has the pandemic hurt K-12 learning? Let state testing in the spring tell us, *The Washington Post*, washingtonpost.com/opinions/2020/11/25/how-badly-has-pandemic-hurt-k-12-learning-let-state-testing-spring-tell-us/; Jimenez, L. (2020) Student assessment during COVID-19, *Center for American Progress*, americanprogress.org/issues/education-k-12/reports/2020/09/10/490209/student-assessment-covid-19/; Tucker, M. (2020) COVID-19 and our schools: The real challenge, *Tucker's Blog*, National Center for Education and the Economy, Washington, DC, ncee.org/2020/06/covid-19-and-our-schools-the-real-challenge/; Washington Post Editorial Board (2021) Why we shouldn't abandon student testing this spring, *Washington Post*, washingtonpost.com/opinions/why-we-shouldnt-abandon-student-testing-this-spring/2021/01/08/839eb860-4ed4-11eb-83e3-322644d82356_story.html; Vaillancourt, T. (Ed) (2021) *Children and schools during COVID-19 and beyond: Engagement and connection through opportunity*, Royal Society COVID-19 Working Group on Children and Schools, Ottawa: Royal Society of Canada.

11 Hargreaves, A. (2021) What the COVID-19 pandemic has taught us about teachers and teaching, *FACETS* 6: 1–28. DOI: 10.1139/facets-2021–0084.

12 Shirley, D., & Hargreaves, A. (2021) *Five paths of student engagement: Blazing the trail to learning and success*, Bloomington: Solution Tree.

13 Hargreaves, A. (2020) Large-scale assessments and their effects: The case of mid-stakes tests in Ontario. *Journal of Educational Change*, 21: 393–420. DOI: 10.1007/s10833-020-09380-5.

14 Buck N. (2020) Children face a deluge of excess screen time – inside the classroom, *Globe and Mail*, theglobeandmail.com/opinion/article-children-face-a-deluge-of-excess-screen-time-inside-the-classroom/; Canadian Pediatric Society (2019) *Digital media: Promoting healthy screen use in school-aged children and adolescents*, cps.ca/en/documents/position/digital-media; McGinn, D. (2020) Parents struggle to wean children

off "perfect storm" of screen time during pandemic, *The Globe and Mail*, theglobeandmail.com/canada/article-parents-struggle-to-wean-children-off-perfect-storm-of-screen-time/; Nature Canada (2018) *Screen time vs green time: The health impacts of too much screen time*, Ottawa, naturecanada.ca/wp-content/uploads/2018/12/NOV-23-FINAL-Contact-Info-Nature-Canada-report-Screen-Time-vs-Green-Time.pdf

15 Henry, J. (2022) 'Writing has dropped off a cliff': England's lockdown-hit pupils get extra pen lessons, *The Guardian*, 23 July, https://www.theguard ian.com/education/2022/jul/23/writing-has-dropped-off-a-cliff-eng lands-lockdown-hit-pupils-get-extra-pen-lessons

16 See https://chenine.ca/about/

17 Kellerman, B. (2004) *Bad leadership: What it is, how it happens, why it matters*, Cambridge, MA: Harvard Business School Press.

18 Kets de Vries, M. (2006) *The leader on the couch: A clinical approach to changing people and organizations*, San Francisco: Wiley.

19 Leithwood, K. (2013) *Strong districts and their leadership*, paper commissioned by The Council for Ontario Directors of Education and the Institute for Educational Leadership, http://www.ontariodirectors.ca/downloads/Strong%20Districts-2.pdf

20 Bauman, Z. (2016) *Strangers at our door*, Oxford: Polity Press.

21 American Psychiatric Association (2013) *Diagnostic and statistical manual of mental disorders* (4th edn), p. 714.

22 Soriano, K. (2022) Tell me all I need to know about narcissistic personality disorder, *Psycom*, 28 October, https://www.psycom.net/personality-disorders/narcissistic

23 Kets de Vries, M. (2006) *The leader on the couch: A clinical approach to changing people and organizations*, San Francisco: Wiley.

24 Storr, A. (1996) *Feet of clay: Saints, sinners and madmen, a study of gurus*, New York: Free Press.

25 *The Sea Beast* (2022) Dir. Chris Williams. Written by Nell Benjamin. Produced by Jed Schlanger, Netflix Animation.

26 Huq, R. (2022) Johnson's war on woke in parliament is a shabby attempt to save his skin, *The Guardian*, 9 February, https://www.theguardian.com/commentisfree/2022/feb/09/boris-johnson-war-on-woke-parliament-mps-unconscious-bias-racism-westminster; Ng, K. (2021) What is the history of the word "woke" and its modern uses? *The Independent*, 22 January, https://www.independent.co.uk/news/uk/home-news/woke-meaning-word-history-b1790787.html

27 Gross, J. (2022) School board in Tennessee bans teaching of Holocaust novel "Maus", *New York Times*, 27 January, https://www.nytimes.com/2022/01/27/us/maus-banned-holocaust-tennessee.html

28 Holiday, R. (2014) *The obstacle is the way: The timeless art of turning trials into triumph*, New York: Portfolio, Penguin, Random House.

29 Robinson, K. (2006) *Do schools kill creativity?* [video file], www.ted.com/talks/sir_ken_robinson_do_schools_kill_creativity?language=en

30 Sarason, S.B. (1982) *The culture of the school and the problem of change* (2nd edn), Boston: Allyn & Bacon, p. 71.

31 Sarason, S.B. (1988) *The making of an American psychologist: An autobiography*, San Francisco: Jossey-Bass, p. 17; Hargreaves, A. (2020) *Moving: A memoir of education and social mobility*, Bloomington: Solution Tree.

32 Gardner, H. (2020) *A synthesizing mind: A memoir from the creator of multiple intelligences theory*, Cambridge, MA: MIT Press.

33 Giridharadas, A. (2019) *Winners take all: The elite charade of changing the world*, New York: Alfred Knopf, pp. 122–123.

34 Wheeler, B. (2019) Brexit sparks boom in applications for politics courses, *BBC*, 27 October, https://www.bbc.com/news/uk-politics-50071242

35 See, for example, Fassassi, I. (2019) Donald Trump and constitutional law, *The Tocqueville Review/La revue Tocqueville* 40(2): 325–338, https://www.muse.jhu.edu/article/743248

36 Lynch, K. & Deegan, P. (2020) Five implications of COVID-19 for Canada and the world, *Globe and Mail*, 1 April, https://www.theglobe andmail.com/business/commentary/article-five-lasting-implications-of-covid-19-for-canada-and-the-world/

37 I first set out these arguments and their implications for education in Hargreaves, A. (2020) What's next for schools after coronavirus? Here are 5 big issues and opportunities, *The Conversation*, 16 April, https://thecon versation.com/whats-next-for-schools-after-coronavirus-here-are-5-big-issues-and-opportunities-135004

38 Iceland's commitment to vocational education as a priority was reflected in its inclusion as part of one of its five pillars of transformation – skills for the future – for its Education 2030 strategy. See OECD (2021) *Iceland education policy 2030 and its implementation*, OECD Education Policy Perspectives, Paris: OECD, https://www.oecd.org/fr/education/iceland-education-policy-2030-and-its-implementation-6e9d2811-en.htm

39 O'Brien, C. (2018) Grind schools record surge in enrolment, *Irish Times*, 3 September, https://www.irishtimes.com/news/education/grind-schools-record-surge-in-enrolment-1.3615888. Note that the OECD report to which I contributed is awaiting a title and publication details at the time this book goes to press.

40 O'Brien, C. (2022) Major changes to Leaving Cert will see students sit some exams in fifth year, *Irish Times*, 29 March, https://www.irishtimes.com/news/education/major-changes-to-leaving-cert-will-see-students-sit-some-exams-in-fifth-year-1.4839186

41 See, for example, Nova Scotia Education and Early Childhood Development (2021) *New outdoor learning fund for Nova Scotia's elementary schools*, Halifax: Government of Nova Scotia, novascotia.ca/news/release/?id=20210413001

42 See, for example, teachers' reactions to the government of Alberta's imposition of a new controversial curriculum in the middle of the pandemic.

Alberta Teachers Association (2021) *Reporting on the third acute wave of Covid-19 in Alberta K-12 schools*, spring, Users/hargrean/Desktop/RSC%20draft/Reporting-on-the-Third-Acute-Wave-of-COVID-19-in-Alberta-Schools-Spring-2021%20(1).pdf

43 OECD (2020) *Education and COVID-19: Focusing on the long-term impact of school closures*, oecd.org/coronavirus/policy-responses/education-and-covid-19-focusing-on-the-long-term-impact-of-school-closures-2cea926e/

44 Education Scotland (2021) *What Scotland learned: Building back better*, Livingstone, education.gov.scot/media/nwibvl2q/what-scotland-learned-building-back-better.pdf

45 Education Scotland (2021) *What Scotland learned: Building back better*, Livingstone, education.gov.scot/media/nwibvl2q/what-scotland-learned-building-back-better.pdf

Chapter 2: Leadership Paradoxes

1 Munby, S. (2019) *Imperfect leadership: A book for leaders who know they don't know it all*, Carmarthen: Crown House Publishing.

2 Munby, S., & Bretherton, M.-C. (2022) *Imperfect leadership in action*, Carmarthen: Crown House Publishing, p. 7.

3 Cohen, L. (1992) *Anthem*, Stranger Music.

4 Voltaire (1772) *La Beguele, Conte Moral*, reprinted by Kessinger Publishing (2009).

5 Smith, A.W. (2013) *Overcoming perfectionism: Finding the key to balance and self-acceptance*, Deerfield Beach: Health Communications Inc.

6 Dewey, J. (1916) *Democracy and education*, New York: Free Press, p. 137.

7 Dewey, J. (1916) *Democracy and education*, New York: Free Press, p. 205.

8 Dewey, J. (1916) *Democracy and education*, New York: Free Press, p. 204.

9 Dewey, J. (1916) *Democracy and education*, New York: Free Press, p. 205.

10 Munby, S. (2019) *Imperfect leadership: A book for leaders who know they don't know it all*, Carmarthen: Crown House Publishing, p. 131.

11 Munby, S. (2019) *Imperfect leadership: A book for leaders who know they don't know it all*, Carmarthen: Crown House Publishing, p. 158.

12 Munby, S. (2019) *Imperfect leadership: A book for leaders who know they don't know it all*, Carmarthen: Crown House Publishing, p. 158.

13 The nature and origin of LEGO's interpretation of the paradoxes of leadership is described more fully in Luscher, L.S. (2018) *Managing leadership paradoxes*, New York: Routledge.

14 "It's hard to be humble song", written and recorded by Matt Davis (1980), from the LP *It's hard to be humble*, RCA Records.

15 Luscher, L.S., & Lewis, M.W. (2008) Organizational change and managerial sensemaking: Working through paradox, *Academy of Management Journal* 51(2), https://doi.org/10.5465/amj.2008.31767217

16 Ng, P.T. (2017) *Learning from Singapore: The power of paradoxes*, New York: Routledge.

17 Fullan, M. (1994) Co-ordinating top-down and bottom-up strategies for educational reform, in Anson, R.J. (Ed) *Systemic reform: Perspectives on personalizing education*, Ann Arbor: University of Michigan Library, p. 1, http://michaelfullan.ca/wp-content/uploads/2016/06/13396035630.pdf

18 Fullan, M. (1994) Co-ordinating top-down and bottom-up strategies for educational reform, in Anson, R.J. (Ed) *Systemic reform: Perspectives on personalizing education*, Ann Arbor: University of Michigan Library, p. 3, http://michaelfullan.ca/wp-content/uploads/2016/06/133960356 30.pdf

19 Fullan, M., Hill, P., & Crévola, C. (2006) *Breakthrough*, Thousand Oaks: Corwin.

20 Fullan, M., & Rincón-Gallardo, S. (2016) Developing high quality public education in Canada: The case of Ontario, in Adamson, F., Astrand, B., & Darling-Hammond, L. (Eds) *Global education reform: How privatization and public investment influence education outcomes*, New York: Routledge.

21 Fullan, M., & Quinn, J. (2015) *Coherence: The right drivers in action for schools, districts, and systems*, Thousand Oaks: Corwin.

22 Elmore, R. (2016) "Getting to scale . . ." it seemed like a good idea at the time, *Journal of Educational Change* 17(4): 529–537.

23 Gross, N., Giacquinta, J.B., & Bernstein, M. (1971) *Implementing organizational innovations: A sociological analysis of planned educational change*, New York: Basic Books; Loucks, S.F., & Hall, G.E. (1977) Assessing and facilitating the implementation of innovations: A new approach, *Educational Technology* 17(2): 18–21.

24 Anderson, S.E. (2010) Moving change: Evolutionary perspectives on educational change, in Hargreaves, A., Fullan, M., Lieberman, A., & Datnow, A. (Eds) *The second international handbook of educational change*, Dordrecht: Springer, pp. 65–84.

25 Chen, J.-O., Moran, S., & Gardner, H. (Eds) (2009) *Multiple intelligences around the world*, San Francisco: Jossey-Bass.

26 Giles, C., & Hargreaves, A. (2006) The sustainability of innovative schools as learning organizations and professional learning communities during standardized reform, *Educational Administration Quarterly* 42(1): 124–156.

27 Mehta, J., & Fine, S. (2019) *In search of deep learning: The quest to remake the American high school*, Cambridge, MA: Harvard University Press.

28 Hatch, T. (2022) *The education we need for a future we can't predict*, New York: Teachers College Press.

29 Hargreaves, A., & Fink, D. (2006) *Sustainable leadership*, San Francisco: Wiley.

30 Hargreaves, A., & Shirley, D. (2009) *The fourth way*, Thousand Oaks: Corwin, p. 10.

31 Hatch, T. (2022) *The education we need for a future we can't predict*, New York: Teachers College Press, p. xxviii.

32 Hatch, T. (2022) *The education we need for a future we can't predict*, New York: Teachers College Press, p. 9.

33 Milkman, H. (2016) Iceland succeeds at reversing teenage substance abuse the US should follow suit, *Huffington Post*, 6 December, https://www.huff post.com/entry/iceland-succeeds-at-rever_b_9892758

34 Roonema, M. (2017) Global lessons from Estonia's tech-savvy government, *UNESCO Courier*, April–June, https://en.unesco.org/courier/2017-april-june/global-lessons-estonia-s-tech-savvy-government; Gouëdard, P., Pont, B., & Viennet, R. (2020) *Education responses to COVID-19: Implementing a way forward*, OECD Education Working Papers, No. 224, Paris: OECD Publishing, https://doi.org/10.1787/8e95f977-en

35 ARC Education Project (2020) System highlights: Uruguay, http://atrico. org/wp-content/uploads/2020/04/COVID-19-in-Uruguay-Educa tional-Disruption-and-Response.pptx.pdf

36 Hatch, T. (2022) *The education we need for a future we can't predict*, New York: Teachers College Press, p. 7.

37 This was part of UN General Assembly, *Transforming our world: The 2030 Agenda for Sustainable Development*, 21 October 2015, A/RES/70/1, https://www.refworld.org/docid/57b6e3e44.html

38 OECD (2018) *Global competency for an inclusive world*, Paris: OECD, https://www.oecd.org/education/Global-competency-for-an-inclusive-world.pdf

39 www.atrico.org

40 ASCD (2020) *The learning compact renewed: Whole child for the whole world*, p. 28; ASCD (n.d.) *The whole child approach to education*, http://files.ascd. org/pdfs/programs/WholeChildNetwork/2020-whole-child-network-learning-compact-renewed.pdf

41 Kilpatrick, W.H. (1918) The project method, *Teachers College Record* 19(4): 319–336.

42 Central Advisory Council for Education (1967) *Children and their primary schools (the Plowden Report)* (Vol. 1), London: HMSO.

43 Schwartz, B. (2004) *The paradox of choice: Why more is less*, New York: HarperCollins.

44 For more on these uses of transparency see the index produced by Transparency International (2014) The 2012 corruption perceptions index measures the perceived levels of public sector corruption in 175 countries and territories, https://www.transparency.org/cpi2014

45 See Hattie, J. (2013) *Visible learning: A synthesis of over 800 meta-analyses relating to achievement*, London: Routledge. Also, DuFour, R., DuFour, R.B., & Eaker, R.E. (2008) *Revisiting professional learning communities at work: New insights for improving schools*, Bloomington: Solution Tree.

46 Datnow, A., & Park, V. (2014) *Data-driven leadership*, San Francisco: Jossey-Bass/Wiley Inc.; Datnow, A., & Park, V. (2019) *Professional*

collaboration with purpose: Teacher learning for equitable and excellent schools, New York: Routledge.

47 See, for example, Fullan, M. (2011) *The six secrets of change: What the best leaders do to help their organizations survive and thrive*, Malden: John Wiley & Sons.

48 Mann, S., Nolan, J., & Wellman, B. (2002) Sousveillance: Inventing and using wearable computing devices for data collection in surveillance environments, *Surveillance & Society* 1(3): 331–355.

Chapter 3: Leading In the Middle

1 Mourshed, M., Chijioke, C., & Barber, M. (2011) How the world's most improved school systems keep getting better, *Educational Studies* 1: 7–25.

2 Johnson, S.M., Marietta, G., Higgins, M.C., Mapp, K.L., & Grossman, A. (2015) *Achieving coherence in district improvement: Managing the relationship between the central office and schools*, Cambridge, MA: Harvard Education Press.

3 For more details of our research on Tower Hamlets, see Hargreaves, A., & Shirley, D. (2012) *The global fourth way*, Thousand Oaks: Corwin. Our research on Hackney is reported in Hargreaves, A., Boyle, A., & Harris, A. (2014) *Uplifting leadership: How teams, and communities raise performance*, San Francisco: Jossey-Bass.

4 Noguera, P.A. (2017) Introduction to "racial inequality and education: Patterns and prospects for the future", *The Educational Forum* 81(2): 129–135, DOI: 10.1080/00131725.2017.1280753

5 Smith, H. (2022) It's time to eliminate school boards, *Education Next*, October, https://www.educationnext.org/its-time-to-eliminate-school-boards/

6 Zimmerman, J. (2021) Why the culture wars in schools are worse than ever before, *Politico*, 19 September, https://www.politico.com/news/magazine/2021/09/19/history-culture-wars-schools-america-divided-512614

7 See https://www.nj.gov/education/doedata/fact.shtml

8 OECD (2016) *Reviews of school resources: Czech Republic*, Paris: OECD, https://www.oecd-ilibrary.org/docserver/9789264262379-5-en.pdf?expires=1671183256&id=id&accname=guest&checksum=4BC21F6F61A31A5144DC5E08A9DE9C88

9 OECD (2017) *The funding of school education: Connecting resources and learning. Iceland*, Paris: OECD, https://www.oecd.org/education/school/AnnexA_Iceland_CountryProfile.pdf

10 Glaze, A. (2018) *Raise the bar: A coherent and responsive education administrative system for Nova Scotia*, https://www.ednet.ns.ca/docs/raisethebar-en.pdf

11 Glaze, A. (2018) *Raise the bar: A coherent and responsive education administrative system for Nova Scotia*, https://www.ednet.ns.ca/docs/raisethebar-en.pdf, p. 23.

12 Glaze, A. (2018) *Raise the bar: A coherent and responsive education administrative system for Nova Scotia*, https://www.ednet.ns.ca/docs/raisethebar-en.pdf, p. 23.

13 Glaze, A. (2018) *Raise the bar: A coherent and responsive education administrative system for Nova Scotia*, https://www.ednet.ns.ca/docs/raisethebar-en.pdf, p. 24.

14 Ravitch, D. (2020) *Slaying Goliath: The passionate resistance to privatization and the fight to save America's public schools*, New York: Knopf.

15 Gleason, P., Clark, M., Tuttle, C.C., & Dwoyer, E. (2010) *The evaluation of charter school impacts: Final report*, Jessup: National Center for Education Evaluation and Regional Assistance.

16 National Conference of State Legislatures (n.d.) Research, Washington, DC, https://www.ncsl.org/research/education/charter-schools-research-and-report.aspx

17 Ladd, H.F., & Fiske, E.B. (2016) *England confronts the limits of school autonomy*, National Center for the Study of Privatization in Education [NCSPE] Working Paper No. 232, New York: Teachers College, Columbia University.

18 Hutchings, M., Francis, B., & Kirby, P. (2015) *Chain effects 2015: The impact of academy chains on low-income students*, London: Sutton Trust.

19 Ladd, H.F., & Fiske, E.B. (2016) *England confronts the limits of school autonomy*, National Center for the Study of Privatization in Education [NCSPE] Working Paper No. 232, New York: Teachers College, Columbia University.

20 Bhattacharya, A. (2021) How much choice is enough? Parental satisfaction with secondary school choice in England and Scotland, *Journal of Social Policy*, 1–21. DOI: https://doi.org/10.1017/S00472 7942100091X

21 Wiborg, S. (2014) The big winners from Sweden's for-profit 'free' schools are companies, not pupils, *The Conversation*, 9 September.

22 Hargreaves, A. (2016) *Teachers and professional collaboration: How Sweden has become the ABBA of educational change*, Albert Shanker Institute, 2 March, http://www.shankerinstitute.org/blog/teachers-and-professional-collaboration-how-sweden-has-become-abba-educational-change; and Hjelm, S. (2020) Vouchers and market-driven schools in Sweden, *Larry Cuban on School Reform and Classroom Practice*, https://larrycuban.word press.com/2020/12/31/vouchers-and-market-driven-schools-in-sweden-sara-hjelm/

23 OECD (2012) *Improving schools in Sweden*, Paris: OECD, https://www.oecd.org/education/school/Improving-Schools-in-Sweden.pdf

24 Skolverket (2010) *What influences educational achievement in Swedish schools?* Stockholm, https://www.skolverket.se/publikationsserier/ovrigt-material/2010/what-influences-educational-achievement-in-swedish-schools; Sahlgren, G.H. (2016) *Regulation and funding of independent*

schools: Lessons from Sweden, Vancouver: Fraser Institute, https://www.fra
serinstitute.org/sites/default/files/regulation-and-funding-of-independ
ent-schools-lessons-from-sweden.pdf

25 Barber, M., & Day, S. (2014) *The new opportunity to lead: A vision for education in Massachusetts in the next 20 years*, Boston: Massachusetts Business
Alliance for Education.

26 Fullan, M. (2015) Leadership from the middle, *Education Canada* 55(4):
22–26.

27 Schleicher, A. (2015) *Schools for 21st-century learners: Strong leaders, confident teachers, innovative approaches*, Paris: OECD.

28 Whitley, J., & Hargreaves, A. (2020) *Interim report of the developmental
evaluation of the implementation of the Nova Scotia Inclusive Education
Policy*, Ottawa, University of Ottawa.

29 Greany, T., & Higham, R. (2018) *Hierarchy, markets and networks:
Analysing the "self-improving school-led system" agenda in England and the
implications for schools*, London: UCL Institute of Education Press.

30 Greany, T., & Higham, R. (2018) *Hierarchy, markets and networks:
Analysing the "self-improving school-led system" agenda in England and the
implications for schools*, London: UCL Institute of Education Press.

31 Greany, T., & Higham, R. (2018) *Hierarchy, markets and networks:
Analysing the "self-improving school-led system" agenda in England and the
implications for schools*, London: UCL Institute of Education Press.

32 Greany, T., & Higham, R. (2018) *Hierarchy, markets and networks:
Analysing the "self-improving school-led system" agenda in England and the
implications for schools*, London: UCL Institute of Education Press.

Chapter 4: Leading Districts From the Middle

1 Kraut, R. (2022) Aristotle's ethics, in Zalta, E.N., & Nodelman,
U. (Eds) *The Stanford encyclopedia of philosophy*, https://plato.stanford.edu/
archives/fall2022/entries/aristotle-ethics/

2 Hargreaves, A., Braun, H.I., Hughes, M., Chapman, L., Lam, K., Lee, Y.,
Morton, B., Sallis, K., Steiner, A., & Welch, M. (2012) *Leading for all:
A research report on the development, design, implementation, and impact of
Ontario's "Essential for some, good for all" initiative*, Ontario: Council of
Directors of Education.

3 Hargreaves, A., Shirley, D., Wangia, S., Bacon, C.K., & D'Angelo, M.
(2018) *Leading from the middle: Spreading learning, well-being, and identity
across Ontario*, Ontario: Council of Directors of Education.

4 For further details on the project methodology, read Hargreaves, A.
(2020) Large-scale assessments and their effects: The case of mid-stakes
tests in Ontario, *Journal of Educational Change* 21: 393–420, https://
doi.org/10.1007/s10833-020-09380-5; Shirley, D., Hargreaves, A., &
Washington, S. (2020) The sustainability and non-sustainability of

teachers' and leaders' wellbeing, *Teaching and Teacher Education*, March, https://doi.org/10.1016/j.tate.2019.102987; Hargreaves, A., & Shirley, D. (2020) Leading from the middle: Its nature, origins and importance, *Journal of Professional Capital and Community* 5(1): 92–114, https://doi.org/10.1108/JPCC-06-2019-0013.

5 See Hargreaves, A., Braun, H.I., Hughes, M., Chapman, L., Lam, K., Lee, Y., Morton, B., Sallis, K., Steiner, A., & Welch, M. (2012) *Leading for all: A research report on the development, design, implementation, and impact of Ontario's "Essential for some, good for all" initiative*, Ontario: Council of Directors of Education.

6 Further details of this project and its impact can be found in Fullan, M., McEachern, J., & Quinn, J. (2017) *Toward district wide deep learning: A cross case study*, New Pedagogies for Deep Learning, Deep Learning Series, http://npdl.global/wp-content/uploads/2017/01/npdl-case_study_1.pdf; Lieberman, A., Campbell, C., & Yashkina, A. (2016) *Teacher learning and leadership: Of, by, and for teachers*, New York: Taylor & Francis.

7 See Hargreaves, A., Braun, H.I., Hughes, M., Chapman, L., Lam, K., Lee, Y., Morton, B., Sallis, K., Steiner, A., & Welch, M. (2012) *Leading for all: A research report on the development, design, implementation, and impact of Ontario's "Essential for some, good for all" initiative*, Ontario: Council of Directors of Education.

8 See Hargreaves, A., Braun, H.I., Hughes, M., Chapman, L., Lam, K., Lee, Y., Morton, B., Sallis, K., Steiner, A., & Welch, M. (2012) *Leading for all: A research report on the development, design, implementation, and impact of Ontario's "Essential for some, good for all" initiative*, Ontario: Council of Directors of Education.

9 https://campaignforpubliceducation.ca/ontario-school-boards-2/

10 Fraser Institute (2021) School enrolment in Canada, Part 2: More Canadian parents choosing independent schools, 3 February, https://www.fraserinstitute.org/blogs/school-enrolment-in-canada-part-2-more-canadian-parents-choosing-independent-schools

11 See Hargreaves, A., & Shirley, D. (2012) *The global fourth way*, Thousand Oaks: Corwin.

12 Ontario Ministry of Education (2005) *Education for all*, http://www.edu.gov.on.ca/eng/document/reports/speced/panel/speced.txt

13 The pie chart was produced through collaborative discussion with members of the ten consortium boards and is first reported in our second project report. See Hargreaves, A., Braun, H.I., Hughes, M., Chapman, L., Lam, K., Lee, Y., Morton, B., Sallis, K., Steiner, A., & Welch, M. (2012) *Leading for all: A research report on the development, design, implementation, and impact of Ontario's "Essential for some, good for all" initiative*, Ontario: Council of Directors of Education.

14 On the concept of professional capital in education, see Hargreaves, A., & Fullan, M. (2012) *Professional capital: Transforming teaching in every school*, New York: Teachers College Press.

15 Holiday, R. (2014) *The obstacle is the way: The timeless art of turning trials into triumph*, New York: Portfolio, Penguin, Random House.

16 Fullan, M., & Rincón-Gallardo, S. (2016) Developing high quality public education in Canada: The case of Ontario, in Adamson, F., Astrand, B., & Darling-Hammond, L. (Eds) *Global education reform: How privatization and public investment influence education outcomes*, New York: Routledge.

17 Van der Zee, R. (2015) How Amsterdam became the bicycle capital of the world, *The Guardian*, 5 May, https://www.theguardian.com/cit ies/2015/may/05/amsterdam-bicycle-capital-world-transport-cycling-kindermoord; Shorto, R. (2011) The Dutch way: Bicycles and fresh bread, *New York Times*, 30 July, https://www.nytimes.com/2011/07/31/opinion/sunday/the-dutch-way-bicycles-and-fresh-bread.html

18 UNICEF (2020) *Worlds of influence: Understanding what shapes child well-being in rich countries*, Innocenti Report Card 16.

19 The quotation refers to boards, but "districts" is the retained usage here to preserve consistency in the text.

20 Hargreaves, A., & O'Connor, M.T. (2018) *Collaborative professionalism: When teaching together means learning for all*, Thousand Oaks: Corwin.

Chapter 5: Around and About the Middle

1 Examples in 2022 are the prime ministers or their equivalents of Iceland, Denmark, New Zealand, and Scotland, and the deputy prime minister of Canada.

2 Lakoff, G., & Johnson, M. (2003) *Metaphors we live by*, Chicago: University of Chicago Press.

3 Hargreaves, A., & Shirley, D. (2009) *The fourth way: The inspiring future of educational change*, Thousand Oaks: Corwin.

4 Barber, M. (2007) *Instruction to deliver: Tony Blair, public services, and the challenge of achieving targets*, London: Politico.

5 Fullan, M. (1991) *The new meaning of educational change* (2nd edn), New York: Teachers College Press.

6 Robinson, K., & Aronica, L. (2016) *Creative schools: The grassroots revolution that's transforming education*, London: Penguin Books.

7 Robinson, K. (2016) *The need for a new model of education*, video presentation for the Atlantic Rim Collaboratory Education Summit, Iceland, September.

8 Wright, P., & Radford, T. (2022) James Lovelock: Obituary, *The Guardian*, 22 July, https://www.theguardian.com/environment/2022/jul/27/james-lovelock-obituary

9 Reported in Girardet, H. (2022) The loss of Lovelock, *The Ecologist*, 2 August, https://theecologist.org/2022/aug/02/loss-lovelock

10 Hargreaves, A., & Fink, D. (2006) *Sustainable leadership*, San Francisco: Wiley, p. 7.

11 Hargreaves, A., & Fink, D. (2006) *Sustainable leadership*, San Francisco: Wiley, p. 159.

12 Simon, W.M. (1960) Herbert Spencer and the "social organism", *Journal of the History of Ideas* 21(2): 294–299, https://doi.org/10.2307/2708202

13 "Bottom-up", *Merriam-Webster.com Dictionary*, https://www.merriam-webster.com/dictionary/bottom-up

14 "Bottom-up", Cambridge Dictionary, https://dictionary.cambridge.org/dictionary/english/bottom-up

15 *Metropolis* (1927) Dir. Fritz Lang. Written by Thea von Harbou and Fritz Lang. Produced by Erich Pommer. Produced by UFA. Distributed by Parufamet.

16 Huxley, A. (1932) *Brave new world*, New York: Doubleday, Doran & Co.; Orwell, G. (1949) *Nineteen eighty-four*, London. Secker & Warburg; *The Hunger Games* (2012) Dir. Gary Ross. Written by Gary Ross Suzanne Collins and Billy Ray. Produced by Lionsgate; *The Sea Beast* (2022) Dir. Chris Williams. Written by Chris Williams and Neil Benjamin. Produced by Ned Schlanger. Produced and distributed by Netflix.

17 *Metropolis* (1927) Dir. Fritz Lang. Written by Thea von Harbou and Fritz Lang. Produced by Erich Pommer. Produced by UFA. Distributed by Parufamet

18 The Johann Heinrich Pestalozzi Society, https://jhpestalozzi.org/#:~:text=The%20importance%20of%20an%20all,is%20led%20by%20the%20heart

19 Bell, N. (2014) Teaching by the medicine wheel: An Anishnaabe framework for Indigenous education, *EdCan Net*, 9 June, https://www.edcan.ca/articles/teaching-by-the-medicine-wheel/

20 The following quotes are taken from Hargreaves, A., & Ainscow, M. (2015) The top and bottom of leadership and change, *Phi Delta Kappan* 97(3): 42–48.

21 Hargreaves, A., & Ainscow, M. (2015) The top and bottom of leadership and change, *Phi Delta Kappan* 97(3): 42–48.

22 Hargreaves, A. (2014) Building the professional capital for schools to deliver successful change, in *Improving schools in Wales*, Paris: OECD, pp. 64–90.

23 Carr, C., Brown, S., & Morris, M. (2017) *Assessing the contribution of schools challenge Cymru to outcomes achieved by pathways to success schools*, Cardiff: Welsh Government, https://www.gov.wales/sites/default/files/statistics-and-research/2019-05/assessing-contribution-schools-challenge-cymru-outcomes-achieved-pathways-success-schools.pdf

24 Organization for Economic Cooperation and Development (2015) *Improving schools in Scotland: An OECD perspective*, https://www.oecd.org/education/school/Improving-Schools-in-Scotland-An-OECD-Perspective.pdf

25 BBC (2019) Pisa: Mixed report for Scottish education in world rankings, *BBC*, 3 December, https://www.bbc.com/news/uk-scotland-50642855

26 Noguera, P.A. (2017) Introduction to "racial inequality and education: Patterns and prospects for the future", *The Educational Forum* 81(2): 129–135, DOI: 10.1080/00131725.2017.1280753

27 Bugler, D. (2021) *School district collaboration: Lessons from districts participating in California Education Partners' California Language & Learning Initiative (CALLI)*, Alameda: WestEd.

28 Bugler, D. (2021) *School district collaboration: Lessons from districts participating in California Education Partners' California Language & Learning Initiative (CALLI)*, Alameda: WestEd.

29 Knudson, J., & Garibaldi, M. (2015) *None of us are as good as all of us: Early lessons from the CORE districts*, August, San Matteo: American Institutes for Research, https://air.prod.acquia-sites.com/sites/default/files/CORE-Cross-District-Collaboration-Report-August-2015.pdf

Chapter 6: Leading Networks From the Middle

1 Lima, J.Á. (2010) Thinking more deeply about networks in education, *Journal of Educational Change* 11(1): 1–21.

2 Hadfield, M., & Chapman, C. (2009) *Leading school-based networks*, New York: Routledge.

3 Wellman, B. (1983) Network analysis: Some basic principles, *Sociological Theory* 1(1): 155–200.

4 Granovetter, M.S. (1973) The strength of weak ties, *American Journal of Sociology* 78(6): 1360–1380.

5 Little, J.W. (1990) The persistence of privacy: Autonomy and initiative in teachers' professional relations, *Teachers' College Record* 91(4): 509–536.

6 Leslie, I. (2020) Why your "weak-tie" friendships may mean more than you think, *BBC*, 2 July, https://www.bbc.com/worklife/article/20200701-why-your-weak-tie-friendships-may-mean-more-than-you-think#:~:text=Granovetter%20named%20these%20categories%20%E2%80%809Cstrong,jobs%20through%20someone%20they%20knew

7 Mangan, I. (2020) Coronavirus Ireland: An Post workers to check in on elderly amid Covid-19 outbreak, *Irish Mirror*, 25 March, https://www.irishmirror.ie/news/irish-news/coronavirus-ireland-update-post-office-21751921

8 Louis, K.S. (2005) Reconnecting knowledge utilization and school improvement: Two steps forward, one step back, in Hopkins, D. (Ed) *The practice and theory of educational change*, reprinted from *International handbook of educational change*, Dordrecht: Springer, pp 40–61.

9 Louis, K.S. (2005) Reconnecting knowledge utilization and school improvement: Two steps forward, one step back, in Hopkins, D. (Ed) *The practice and theory of educational change*, reprinted from *International handbook of educational change*, Dordrecht: Springer, pp 40–61.

10 Louis, K.S. and Miles, M. (1990) *Improving the urban high school: What works and why*, New York: Teachers College Press.

11 Hatch describes and draws upon these networks in his book Hatch, T. (2022) *The education we need for a future we can't predict*, New York: Teachers College Press.

12 The National School Reform Faculty established and trademarked Critical Friends Groups – see https://nsrfharmony.org/. For research on the National Writing Project in the United States, see Lieberman, A., & Grolnick, M. (1996) Networks and reform in American education, *Teachers College Record* 98(1): 7–45. For information on Big Picture Schools, see https://www.bigpicture.org/schools

13 Castells, M. (1996) *The rise of the network society*, Oxford: Blackwell.

14 See Lima, J.Á. (2010) Thinking more deeply about networks in education, *Journal of Educational Change* 11(1): 1–21.

15 Details of our evaluation of the Raising Achievement, Transforming Learning network are in Hargreaves, A., & Shirley, D. (2009) *The fourth way*, Thousand Oaks: Corwin. Our evaluation of the Alberta Initiative for School Improvement is reported in Hargreaves, A., & Shirley, D. (2012) *The global fourth way*, Thousand Oaks: Corwin. Our work with the NW RISE network in the United States is reported in Hargreaves, A., Parsley, D., & Cox, E. (2015) Designing and launching rural school improvement networks: Aspirations and actualities, *Peabody Journal of Education* 90(2): 306–321 and in Hargreaves, A., & Shirley, D. (2021) The future of learning lies in engagement, *Educational Leadership* 79(4): 26–31, https://www.ascd.org/el/articles/the-future-of-learning-lies-in-engagement. Our work in designing a developing a network of schools using playful learning for minoritized populations of students is reported at the end of this chapter and is also available at www.playjouer.ca

16 For more details of our research on Tower Hamlets, see Hargreaves, A., & Shirley, D. (2009) *The fourth way*, Thousand Oaks: Corwin.

17 Our research on Hackney is reported in Hargreaves, A., Boyle, A., & Harris, A. (2014) *Uplifting leadership: How teams, and communities raise performance*, San Francisco: Jossey-Bass.

18 This work is reported in detail in Hargreaves, A., & Shirley, D. (2009) *The fourth way*, Thousand Oaks: Corwin, and in Evans, M.P., & Stone-Johnson, C. (2010) Internal leadership challenges of network participation, *International Journal of Leadership in Education*, 13(2): 203–220, DOI: 10.1080/13603120903288405

19 Armstrong, P.A., Brown, C., & Chapman, C.J. (2020) School-to-school collaboration in England: A configurative review of the empirical evidence, *Review of Education* 9(1): 319–351, https://doi.org/10.1002/rev3.3248

20 For information on the Coalition of Essential Schools, go to http://essentialschools.org/. Details of the New Pedagogies for Deep Learning network can be found at https://deep-learning.global/

21 Muncey, D., & McQuillan, P. (1996) *Reform and resistance in schools and classrooms: An ethnographic view of the coalition of essential schools*, New Haven: Yale University Press; Datnow, A., & Murphy, J. (2002) *Leadership lessons from comprehensive schools reform*, Thousand Oaks: Corwin; Datnow, A., Borman, G.D., Stringfield, S., Overman, L.T., & Castellano, M. (2003) Comprehensive school reform in culturally and linguistically diverse contexts: Implementation and outcomes from a four-year study, *Educational Evaluation and Policy Analysis*, 25(2): 143–170, https://doi.org/10.3102/01623737025002143; Datnow, A. (2005) The sustainability of comprehensive school reform models in changing district and state contexts, *Educational Administration Quarterly* 41(1): 121–153, https://doi.org/10.1177/0013161X04269578

22 Arnold, K., & Mihut, G. (2020) Postsecondary outcomes of innovative high schools: The big picture longitudinal study, *Teachers College Record* 122(8): 1–42, https://doi.org/10.1177/016146812012200803

23 Arnold, K., & Mihut, G. (2020) Postsecondary outcomes of innovative high schools: The big picture longitudinal study, *Teachers College Record* 122(8): 1–42, https://doi.org/10.1177/016146812012200803

24 Arnold, K., & Mihut, G. (2020) Postsecondary outcomes of innovative high schools: The big picture longitudinal study, *Teachers College Record* 122(8): 1–42, https://doi.org/10.1177/016146812012200803

25 Arnold, K., & Mihut, G. (2020) Postsecondary outcomes of innovative high schools: The big picture longitudinal study, *Teachers College Record* 122(8): 1–42, https://doi.org/10.1177/016146812012200803

26 Hargreaves, A., & Shirley, D. (2012) *The global fourth way*, Thousand Oaks: Corwin.

27 Hargreaves, A., Parsley, D., & Cox, E. (2015) Designing and launching rural school improvement networks: Aspirations and actualities, *Peabody Journal of Education* 90(2): 306–321.

28 Hargreaves, A., & Shirley, D. (2021) The future of learning lies in engagement, *Educational Leadership* 79(4): 26–31, https://www.ascd.org/el/articles/the-future-of-learning-lies-in-engagement

29 See Hargreaves, A., Parsley, D., & Cox, E. (2015) Designing and launching rural school improvement networks: Aspirations and actualities, *Peabody Journal of Education* 90(2): 306–321; Lima, J.Á. (2010) Thinking more deeply about networks in education, *Journal of Educational Change* 11(1): 1–21; Daly, A. (Ed.) (2010) *Social network theory and educational change*, Cambridge, MA: Harvard Education Press.

30 Hadfield, M., & Chapman, C. (2009) *Leading school-based networks*, New York: Routledge.

31 One of the best examples of an assessment-based network is the New York Performance Assessment Consortium. Details are available at http://www.performanceassessment.org/

32 Sarason, S.B. (1972) *The creation of settings and the future societies*, San Francisco: Jossey-Bass.

33 Sarason, S.B. (1972) *The creation of settings and the future societies*, San Francisco: Jossey-Bass.

34 Depeche Mode (1981) *Just Can't Get Enough*. Written by Vince Clarke. Released by Mute. Produced by Depeche Mode and Daniel Miller. Recorded at Blackwing Studios, London.

35 Busher, H., & Hodgkinson, K. (1995) Managing interschool networks: Across the primary/secondary divide, *School Organisation* 15(3): 329–340.

36 Evans, M., & Stone-Johnson, C. (2011) Internal leadership challenges of network participation, *International Journal of Leadership in Education* 13(2): 203–220.

37 *Succession* (2018) HBO TV drama series. Created by Jesse Armstrong. Distributed by Warner Brothers.

38 See https://learningthroughplay.com/

39 www.playjouer.ca

40 The 13 international advisers are listed at https://playjouer.ca/team-cate gory/international-advisors/

Chapter 7: Leading Systems From the Middle

1 Wilkinson, R., & Pickett, K. (2009) *The spirit level: Why greater equality makes societies stronger*, London and New York: Bloomsbury; Wilkinson, R., & Pickett, K. (2018) *The inner level: How more equal societies reduce stress, restore sanity, and improve everyone's well-being*, New York: Penguin.

2 Hargreaves, A. (2002) Teaching and betrayal, *Teachers and Teaching* 8(3): 393–407, DOI: 10.1080/135406002100000521

3 Sahlberg, P. (2011) The fourth way of Finland, *Journal of Educational Change* 12(2): 173–185, https://pasisahlberg.com/wp-content/uploads/2013/01/ The-Fourth-Way-of-Finland-JEC-2011.pdf; Sahlberg, P. (2021) *Finnish lessons 3.0: What can the world learn from educational change in Finland?* New York: Teachers College Press.

4 Hargreaves, A., Halasz, G., & Pont, B. (2008) The Finnish approach to system leadership, in Pont, B., Nusche, D., & Hopkins, D. (Eds) *Improving school leadership, volume 2, case studies on system leadership*, Paris: OECD, pp. 69–109.

5 Sahlberg, P., & Walker, T.D. (2021) *In teachers we trust: The Finnish way to world class schools*, New York: Norton.

6 Sahlberg, P. (2009) *A short history of educational reform in Finland*, Turin: European Training Foundation, p. 27, https://www.disal.it/Resource/ Finland-Sahlberg.pdf

7 Salbo, P., & Torbjorn, S. (2016) Finland: Trust under pressure, in Fink, D. (Ed) *Trust and verify: The real keys to school improvement*, London. UCL Institute of Education Press.

8 Hargreaves, D.H. (2019) *Beyond schooling: An anarchist challenge*, London: Routledge.

9 Hargreaves, D.H. (2019) *Beyond schooling: An anarchist challenge*, London: Routledge.

10 Hargreaves, D.H. (2019) *Beyond schooling: An anarchist challenge*, London: Routledge.

11 See, for example, the expert chapters that make up the report for the Canadian Royal Society on COVID-19 and schools in Vaillancourt, T. (Ed.) (2021) *Children and schools during Covid-19 and beyond: Engagement and connection through opportunity*, Ottawa: Royal Society of Canada.

12 Hargreaves, D.H. (2019) *Beyond schooling: An anarchist challenge*, London: Routledge.

13 See Cabinet Office (2006) *The UK government's approach to public service reform*, London: Cabinet Office. The first of a series of think pieces by David Hargreaves, for what was then the UK government's National College for Leadership of Schools and Children's Services, was published in 2010. See Hargreaves, D. (2010) *Creating a self-improving school system*, Nottingham: NCSL, https://assets.publishing.service.gov.uk/government/uploads/system/uploads/attachment_data/file/325873/creating-a-self-improving-school-system.pdf

14 Greany, T., & Higham, R. (2018) *Hierarchy, markets and networks: Analysing the "self-improving school-led system" agenda in England and the implications for schools*, London: UCL Institute of Education Press.

15 Greany, T., & Higham, R. (2018) *Hierarchy, markets and networks: Analysing the "self-improving school-led system" agenda in England and the implications for schools*, London: UCL Institute of Education Press.

16 Greany, T., & Higham, R. (2018) *Hierarchy, markets and networks: Analysing the "self-improving school-led system" agenda in England and the implications for schools*, London: UCL Institute of Education Press.

17 Greany, T., & Higham, R. (2018) *Hierarchy, markets and networks: Analysing the "self-improving school-led system" agenda in England and the implications for schools*, London: UCL Institute of Education Press.

18 Clark, J.P. (1977) *The philosophical anarchism of William Godwin*, Princeton: Princeton University Press.

19 Supovitz, J. (2014) *Building a lattice for school leadership: The top-to-bottom rethinking of leadership development in England and what it might mean for American education*, Philadelphia: Consortium for Policy Research in Education.

20 Supovitz, J. (2014) *Building a lattice for school leadership: The top-to-bottom rethinking of leadership development in England and what it might mean for American education*, Philadelphia: Consortium for Policy Research in Education.

21 Byrne, P. (1997) *Social movements in Britain*, New York: Routledge.

22 Shirley, D. (1997) *Community organizing for urban school reform*, Austin: University of Texas Press.

23 Rincón-Gallardo, S. (2019) *Liberating learning: Educational change as social movement*, New York: Routledge.

24 See Psacharopoulos, G., Rojas, C., & Velez, E. (1992) *Achievement evaluation of Colombia's Escuela Nueva: Is multigrade the answer?* Policy Research Working Papers, http://documents.worldbank.org/curated/en/887031468770448877/pdf/multi-page.pdf. However, a study of Escuela Nueva's impact in Viet Nam after its subsequent expansion there shows less impact, with no evidence of long-term benefits, and only modest gains in cognitive and non-cognitive skills in the short run. See Dang, H.H., Glewwe, P., Lee, J., & Vu, K. (2022) *The impact evaluation of Vietnam's Escuela Nueva (new school) program on students' cognitive and non-cognitive skills*, Bonn: IZA Institute of Labor Economics, https://docs.iza.org/dp15005.pdf - perhaps indicating the decreased likelihood of systematic impact the larger and more culturally diverse a network becomes.

25 Escuela is one of five global examples of collaborative professionalism discussed in my book of case studies with Michael O'Connor. See Hargreaves, A., & O'Connor, M. (2018) *Collaborative professionalism: When teaching together means learning for all*, Thousand Oaks: Corwin.

26 For more details, see www.atrico.org

27 Anna Walentynowicsz, *The spark that led to solidarity. #Poland*, https://poland.pl/history/historical-figures/anna-walentynowicz-spark-led-solidarity/

28 Bee Gees (2001) "Man in the middle". Written by Barry and Maurice Gibb, on the album *This is Where I Came In*. London, Polydor Records.

Epilogue: Your Leadership

1 Hargreaves, A., & Shirley, D. (2022) *Well-being in schools: Three forces that will uplift your students in a volatile world*, Alexandria: ASCD.

2 Mautz, S. (2021) *Leading from the middle: A playbook for managers to influence up, down, and across the organization*, San Francisco: Wiley.

3 See, for example, Harris, A., Jones, M., Ismail, N., & Nguyen, D. (2019) Middle leaders and middle leadership in schools: Exploring the knowledge base (2003–2017), *School Leadership & Management* 39(3–4): 255–277, DOI: 10.1080/13632434.2019.1578738; Day, C., & Grice, C. (2019) *Investigating the influence and impact of leading from the middle: A school-based strategy for middle leaders in schools*, Sydney: Association of Independent Schools Leadership Centre, https://ses.library.usyd.edu.au/handle/2123/19972?show=full; Lipscombe, K., Grice, C., Tindall-Ford, S., & De-Nobile, J. (2020) Middle leading in Australian schools: Professional standards, positions, and professional development, *School Leadership & Management* 40(5): 406–424, DOI: 10.1080/13632434.2020.1731685;

Childress, D., Chimier, C., Jones, C., Page, E., & Tournier, B. (2020) *Change agents: Emerging evidence on instructional leadership at the middle tier*, Paris: UNESCO and London: Education Development Trust, https://unesdoc.unesco.org/ark:/48223/pf0000374918/PDF/374918eng.pdf.multi.page

4 Kets de Vries, M. (2006) *The leader on the couch: A clinical approach to changing people and organizations*, San Francisco: Wiley.

5 Cain, S. (2013) *Quiet: The power of introverts in a world that can't stop talking*, New York: Crown.

Index

Note: Locators in *italic* indicate figures and locators in **bold** indicate tables.